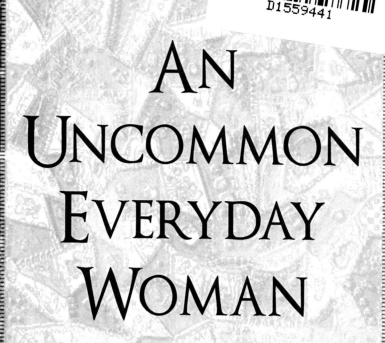

AN UNCOMMON EVERYDAY WOMAN

By Carolyn Kennedy Muka

the Peppertree Press

Sarasota, Florida

This is Carolyn Kennedy Muka's PC.

With this computer I hope to put down the Kennedy-Muka family history. All information forthcoming is subject to my memory and therefore subject to question.

If you find mistakes in this publication, please consider that they are there for a purpose. I am writing something for everyone, and some people are always looking for mistakes.

Carolyn K. Muka, 2003

For information regarding permission,
call 941-922-2662 or contact us at our website:
www.peppertreepublishing.com or write to:
the Peppertree Press, LLC.
Attention: Publisher
1269 First Street, Suite 7
Sarasota, Florida 34236

ISBN: 978-0-9821654-3-0

Library of Congress Number: 2008938570

Printed in the U.S.A.

Printed November 2008

Writing this history has humbled me,
for the lack of skills,
not for the lack of trying.

-CKM

Carolyn at 18

CONTENTS

FAMILY HISTORY

DATES	NAME	NOTES
1/5/39	Patricia Kennedy Sampson	Sister
1/8/62	Magda Gavilonda Muka	Daughter-in-law (James' wife)
1/14/62	Carol Anne Kennedy	Niece (Brother Martin's daughter)
1/19/62	Dooney Stevenson	Sister Marlene's grandson
1/29/62	John Hill	Sister Marlene's son-in-law
2/4/61	Lawrence L. Muka	No. 4 son
2/6/61	Albert Webster Sampson	Sister Patty's son
2/7/25	Richard F. Daly	Friend (died 4/30/97)
2/8/64	Barbara Tomczyk Hill	Niece (Sister Marlene'sdaughter)
2/24/72	Amy Tomczyk	Niece (Sister Marlene's daughter)
2/27/34	Carolyn Joan Kennedy	ME
2/27/66	Nancy Anne Tomczyk	Niece (Sister Marlene's Daughter)
3/12/63	Marion Sampson Toplinski	Niece
3/18/93	Darian Kennedy Muka	Granddaughter
3/26/14	Eleanor Wilcox	Aunt (Died 5/4/94)
4/2/11	Joseph Carroll Kennedy	Father-Died 1/10/41
4/22/88	Taylor Hill	Sister Marlene's Granddaughter
5/5/95	Steven N. Casello	Patty's Grandson

Date	Name	Relation
5/14/11	Marion Wilcox Kennedy Callahan	Mother (Died 5/6/95)
5/20/90	Alexander James Muka	Grandson
6/11/92	Mathew A. Casello	Patty's Grandson
12/20/1881	Stephen Muka	Leonard's Father
7/8/23	Art Tomczyk	Marlene's husband Died
7/16/23	Joseph Carl Kennedy	Nephew (Martin's Son)
7/17/48	Jeffery A. Callahan	Brother
7/27/00	Nathaniel Parrish Muka	Grandson
8/7/36	Marin James Kennedy	Brother (Jimmy)
8/25/59	Michael L. Muka	Son No. 3-Died 12/5/94
8/27/64	James Alan Kennedy	Nephew (Martin's Son)
8/29	Laura Rittman Muka	Daughter-In-Law Lawrence's Wife
8/31/93	Nicholette A. Muka	Granddaughter
	James & Magda	
9/1/66	Margaret Anne Kennedy	Niece Martin's Daughter
9/3/	Marlene & Art Tomczyk	Wedding Anniversary
9/6/	Jason Tomczyk	Marlene's Grandson
9/17/	Joseph Hill	Marlene's Grandson
9/12/82	Kyle Wister	Marlene's Grandson
9/30/	Helen S. Wilcox	Aunt Helen-Uncle Al's Wife
10/3/31	Marlene Kennedy Tomczyk	Sister
1/3/53	Diana Muka	Daughter-Died 12/31/53
10/12/65	Suzanne Sampson Casello	Niece (Patty's Daughter)

10/16/23	Albert Wilcox	Uncle (Uncle Junior)
10/17/23	Leonard Louis Muka	Husband
10/18/54	Stephen L. Muka	Son No.1 (Died 7/11/85)
10/30/30	Joseph C. Kennedy & Marion Wilcox	Parents
10/31/	Clement Wilcox	Uncle (Died 3/15/94)
10/22/90	Christopher M. Casello	Patty's Grandson
11/5/55	Albert & Helen Wilcox	Married
11/11/85	Brittany Laurel Stevenson	Marlene's Granddaughter
11/19/86	Kimberly Muka	Granddaughter-
	Lawrence & Malou	
11/20	Elizabeth Muka (Betty)	Sister-in-law (Died 12/15/93)
11/22/63	J.F. Kennedy	President of USA (Died)
12/23/1878	Martin Kennedy	Grandfather
11/26/	George Sampson & Patty Kennedy	Married
11/17/52	Leonard L. Muka & Carolyn Kennedy	Married (ME)
12/3	Father Bakaisa	Friend – Died 12/3/84
12/8/78	Faye Francisco	Feather-Granddaughter
12/16/63	James Leonard Muka	Son No.5
12/18/61	Maryanne Tomczyk	Marlene's Daughter
12/26/56	Christopher Leonard Muka	Son No.2
12/28/95	Eliot Lawrence Muka	Grandson
	Lawrence & Laura	
12/31/	John Muka	Brother-in-law - Died10/3/85

MUKA TREE ROOTS

PLANTED IN MICHALOVETS IN AUSTRIA-HUNGARY
(AS IT WAS CALLED BACK IN 1881)

Stephen Muka — Born December 20, 1881
He was the oldest of three children.
1. Elizabeth (only sister) died in her 20s.
2. John married Elizabeth Sutack
   (five children) Mary, John, Joseph, Michael and Edward.
3. Stephen Muka (Father of Leonard L. Muka)

Stephen arrived in America around 1896 and settled in
Trenton, NJ. He met Suzanna Adam in December, 1904 and they
were married January 6, 1905 at Ss Peter and Paul's Church.
(At which time it was a little building on Genesse Street, Trenton, NJ).

SUZANNA ADAM
Born to Andrew and Ana Adam in 1879 in Austria-Hungary.

Suzanna arrived in America around 1898
and settled in Trenton, NJ.
She was one of five sisters and one brother:
Anna, Elizabeth, Mary, Suzanna, Helen and Joseph

STEPHEN AND SUZANNA GAVE BIRTH TO FOUR SONS
AND TWO DAUGHTERS:
Mary, Stephen, Joseph (died at 16 months of age),
John, Elizabeth, Leonard and one miscarriage

1. Mary married John Kratzer, Sr. — two sons — Edward died about three weeks after birth. John Peter (Pete) married Margaret Ongrady. They had no children. Pete died 12/10/91. Pete was "Santa" and Margaret is "Margie."

2. Stephen married Veronica Ungrady — two children — Robert (Bob) who had three children and Mary (Little Mary), who had six sons.

3. Joseph died at 16 months old.

4. John married Evelyn Sirovets —three children — Elaine married John Welsch —two sons. John Richard married Patty — two sons, one daughter. Ronald not married yet.
John Sr. died 10/3/85
Elaine died 1999

5. Elizabeth (Known as Old Aunt Betty) — because she was always young and cheerful, never married.

6. Leonard married Carolyn Joan Kennedy — six children
Diane, died 3 months old, 10/3/53 -12/31/53
Stephen, 10/18/54-7/11/85
Christopher, 12/26/56
Michael, 8/25/59 — 12/5/94
Lawrence, 2/4/61
James, 12/16/63Stephen Muka Sr., died 4/21/47

Suzanna Muka, died 1/22/68
Mary Muka Kratzer, died 10/11/53
Stephen Muka Jr., died 12/27/58
John Muka, died 12/3/85
Stephen L. Muka, died 7/11/85
Elizabeth F. Muka, died 12/15/93
Diane Muka, died 12/31/53
Pete Kratzer, died 12/10/91
Michael L. Muka, died 12/5/94

Diane Muka, Stephen L. Muka and Michael L. Muka were
Leonard L Muka and Carolyn Kennedy Muka's children..

LEONARD L. MUKA'S FAMILY

Leonard L. Muka is the baby of his family. As of this date
(1/12/03) he is the only member of his family left alive. His mother
was Suzanna Adam Muka, and his father was Stephen Muka Sr.
Both were born in Austria-Hungary. Suzanna and Stephen had sev-
en children. One baby died very early in life, a second baby boy died
when he was about 16 months old. John, Stephen, Mary, Elizabeth
(Aunt Betty) and Leonard lived to be adults.

Suzanna gave birth to Leonard, her last baby, when she was 44
years old. She lived to see her Leonard turn 44 years of age. Stephen
died at 64 years of age. Leonard's parents married after knowing each
other for only two weeks. It was an arranged marriage. Suzanna was a
housekeeper for a rich lady and as time went by the lady became very
fond of Suzanna and picked out a husband for her. The only require-
ment at the time was that he did not drink alcohol.

John married Evelyn and they had three children. John Richard
(Ricky), Elaine, and Ronald (Ron). Ricky married Patty and they had

11

three children. Elaine married and had two sons. Ronald is single and works in Michigan.

Stephen married Ronnie and they had a son Robert (Bob) and a daughter Mary (Little Mary). Bob had two daughters (both died as adults) and one son. The son and his family used to live up the street from us when we lived at 470 Miller Ave., Trenton, NJ. The daughter Mary was called Little Mary because there was already an older Mary in the family. Mary had six sons.

Mary married a man whose last name was Kratzer. They had two sons, Peter (Pete) also called "Santa Claus." Pete was born on February 27. He and I shared the same birthday with Elizabeth Taylor. Pete married a great gal named Margaret Ongrady, (Margie). The second son died at 3 weeks old.

Elizabeth, (Aunt Betty) never married. She was very fond of her nieces and nephews. Betty was my dear sister-in-law, closer to being one of my sisters. Betty died in our home on December 15, 1993.

Leonard married me, Carolyn Kennedy, on November 27, 1952. We had six beautiful, healthy babies. Diana, Stephen, Christopher, Michael, Lawrence and James.

NOW THE TALE BEGINS

KENNEDY TREE ROOTS

MARION WILCOX KENNEDY CALLAHAN

Marion Rita Wilcox Kennedy married Joseph Carroll Kennedy
on October 30, 1930.four children:
Marlene, October 3, 1931
Carolyn, February 27, 1934
Martin James, August 7,1937
Patricia, January 5, 1939

Joseph Carroll Kennedy died January 10, 1941
(29 years, 9 months old)

Marion Rita Wilcox Kennedy married Jeffrey A. Callahan
one child: Jeffrey A. Callahan Jr., July 17, 1948

Marlene Kennedy married Arthur Tomczyk on September 3
four daughters: Mary Anne, December 18, 1961
Barbara, February 9, 1964
Nancy Anne, February 27, 1966
Amy, February 24, 1972

Carolyn Joan Kennedy married Leonard L. Muka –
November 27, 1952
six children:
Diane,–October 3, 1953 to–December 31, 1953
Stephen, October 18, 1954 to July 11, 1985
Christopher, December 26, 1956
Michael, August 25, 1959 to December 5, 1994
Lawrence, February 4, 1961
James, December 16, 1963

Martin James Kennedy married Patricia Drew
four children:
Joseph, July 16, 1960
Carol, January 14, 1962
James, August 27, 1964
Margaret, September 1, 1966

Patricia Kennedy married George Sampson November 26, 1960
three children:
Albert Webster, February 6, 1961
Marion, March 12, 1963
Suzanne, October 12, 1965
Jeffrey Callahan, not married as of Christmas 2002.

JOSEPH CARROLL KENNEDY

(Carolyn Kennedy Muka's father)

Joseph Carroll Kennedy was my father.
He was called "Carl" by his family.
Born 4/2/1911 —Died 1/10/1941

HIS MOTHER and RELATIVES:
Catherine Coyne Kennedy — 10/23/1884-3/12/1945
Freehold, NJ
Had a twin sister, Mary
Had a sister, Ellen
Had a brother, Joseph

HIS GRANDMOTHER
Mary E. Collins-Died April 1941

HIS GRANDFATHER
Mihael Coyne- Died 1929

HIS GREAT GRANDMOTHER
Bridget Collins Last names were the same-NO relation

HIS GREAT GRANDFATHER
Michael Collins Last names were the same-NO relation

HIS SISTER
Mary Kennedy Born 5/18/1916 Freehold, NJ
Married John K. Barlow
three children:
John K. Barlow, 5/6/41
Martin J. Barlow, 11/3/45
Catherine J. Barlow Danyow, 6/20/49

HIS FATHER and relatives:Martin James Kennedy,
New York City, 12/23/1878 – 3/12/1961
Had two sisters Mary and Nellie (both died in early childhood)
Had two brothers, Michael and Jerry

GRANDMOTHER
Johanna Blood
1840- 1922

GRANDFATHER
Michael Kennedy - Died 1889

Martin and Catherine were married in November 1906
Martin Kennedy child, of Michael Kennedy and Johanna Blood ,
was baptized January 12, 1879 by Rev. T.F. Gregg. Sponsors were
Michael Kennedy and Ellen Hickey at Sacred Heart of Jesus, 457
West 51st St., Borough of Manhattan

DANIEL WEBSTER WILCOX

Daniel Webster Wilcox was born in Wilmington, Mass. April 22, 1858. He died December 25, 1927 (Christmas). He was 69 years old.

Mary Ellen Morris - wife of Daniel Webster Wilcox, was born February 6, 1858 in Wisconsin. She died March 17, 1944. She was 86 years old.

Daniel Webster and Mary Ellen Morris were married at St. Peters Church, Lowell, Mass. on October 6, 1880 by Rev. Peter Crudden, pastor. Hurbert Bisby and Ann Hives witnessed the ceremony. They had twelve children in twenty two years.

CHILDREN: ALL BORN IN LOWELL, MASS
Angeline Wilcox, September 18, 1881-April 20, 1882
Mary E. Wilcox, October 18, 1882-June 12, 1883
Clement Wilcox, June 20, 1884-August 6, 1909
Leo Wilcox, April 21, 1886-November 10, 1968
Albert Webster Wilcox, March 22, 1888-October 8, 1945
Thomas Wilcox, April 11, 1890-May2, 1964
Eva F. Wilcox, September 6, 1891-November 8, 1907
Henry Wilcox, August 10, 1893-May26, 1961
Mary F. Wilcox, March 10, 1896-October 21, 1975
Robert Wilcox, January 17, 1898-March 19,1957
Margaret L. Wilcox, April 51901-December 2, 1980
Loretta E. Wilcox, February 23, 1903-November 1990

This information was given to our family by Mary Ellen Moynihan, daughter of Margaret Wilcox Moynihan (Aunt Peggy to my mom).

I remember going to Lowell and visiting when I was about 12 years of age. I remember Henry and Leo. Aunt Peggy and Loretta came often to Trenton, NJ so they were well known to us kids. Of course, Albert Webster Wilcox was my grandfather and my mother's dad.

Mary and Angelina died as babies.
Clement and Eva died young.
Leo had two daughters.
Albert had five children: Marion (my mom), Eleanor, Clement, Patricia and Albert.
Tom bad no children.
Henry never married.
Mary had two daughters, Genna and Mary.
Robert had one daughter, Anita.
Margaret had one daughter, Mary Ellen, plus one still born baby.
Loretta had two sons, Robert and Richard, plus one daughter Maryann.
Mary (the second one) married John Decker.
Margaret married Corneilus "Neil" Moynihan.
Loretta married Dick O'Malley.

The only grandsons to carry on the Wilcox names were my Uncle Clement and Uncle Albert. They never had any children. This brings an end to the Wilcox name from the union made in October 6, 1880.

MAY MC CARTY

May McCarty married Albert Webster Wilcox. They are the parents of my mother. May was born in 1888. She was one of five children.
Ella married a Qualey and had two children: James (died at 8 years old) and Pauleen. Pauleen married and had a son.
Ella was a seamstress.

Joseph had four children.
Barthalmew
Rose – married Edman Roe. They had no children.
May – married Albert Webster Wilcox. May worked decorating hats in a factory when she was young. They had five children.

1. Marion Wilcox married a Kennedy and a Callahan. She had five children: Marlene Kennedy, Carolyn Kennedy, Martin James Kennedy, Patricia Kennedy and Jeffrey Callahan. Mother died in May 1995.

2. Eleanor was feeble minded after a bad case of measles when she was very young. When a teenager she was put into Vineland State Hospital where she lived to be 80 years old. Died 1994.

3. Clement married May Evens when he was in his 60s. Clement Died March 15, 1994 in Arizona.

4. Patricia married Gene Petrillo. They had three children: Barbara Petrillo Brodbeck (had three children), Patty Petrillo Kelly (had two sons), Gene Jr. (had two children)

5. Albert married Aunt Helen. They had no children

Carolyn at 29

CAROLYN
JOAN KENNEDY

Carolyn Joan Kennedy was born February 27, 1934 at 70 Hull Avenue, Freehold, NJ. Parents were Joseph Carroll Kennedy and Marion Rita Wilcox Kennedy.

I had ears that stuck out and it drove Mother nuts. She is said to have kept a hat on me for the first year of my life so that my ears would lay flat to my head. It didn't work, though, as my ears still stick out - but don't bother me a bit.

My Dad died when I was six years old. This was to be the biggest thing that ruled my life but I had to live my life to finally know this. My Dad's death made my Mother a bitter woman. Her children paid the price day after day. Again, it took a lifetime to see the pattern.

My Dad had a leaky valve in his heart. He had rheumatic fever and there wasn't the type of medicine there is today, so it left him with a bad heart. Dad was 29 years old when he died, but he knew he was going to die two years before it happened. It took the two years to finally fill up his lungs and kill him with his own blood.

Even though I was only six when he died, I remember my Mother telling me where his medicine was, just in case it was needed. Someone else needed to know besides her. Well, my Father asked me one day when he was sick in bed. My Mother had warned me not to let my Dad have his medicine for fear that he would take it all and be done with "this thing called dying." So, of course, I didn't tell my Dad.

I must have been very old for my age. My Mother always used me as the other grown up in the family. In a way I guess it was the right thing to do because it helped me grow up fast and become stable. In the end, I needed all the gifts my parents gave me to make it through this life and help my family.

Mom and Dad had been married ten years and had four children. When he died, Marlene was eight, I was six, Jimmy was four and Patty was two. Patty does not remember much of those days. Marlene and I remember the most. And Jimmy, well, if you can tell by his actions you will see that HE just left our family and never REALLY looked back. Thanks to our Mom.

But back to the grandparents:

Martin J. Kennedy was my Father's Dad.

Catherine Coyne Kennedy was my Father's Mother

Albert Webster Wilcox was my Mother's Dad

May (Mary) McCarty was my Mother's Mother

I remember some, but not a lot about my grandparents. I remember my Grandfather Wilcox making cough medicine with honey and onions (I loved it). I remember him telling me (when I was walking with him in the winter and my hands were cold) to always ware mittens and not gloves. When the fingers were all together they helped keep each other warm. This was in Freehold, NJ, of course. All my grandparents lived and are buried in Freehold.

My Grandmother Wilcox's Mother died from cancer of the nose. I even remember her when she came to visit in Freehold. I was playing with a bat and ball, the little hand-held ones that hold the ball to the bat with a rubber band. My Great Grandmother Wilcox was watching me count how many times I could hit the ball without missing. She was sitting on the front porch of my Grandparents' house and I was at the bottom of the steps. (My Grandparents Wilcox never owned a home, always rented).

My Grandmother Wilcox was a short, stout woman. When she was young and living in Massachusetts she worked making hats in a factory. Because she was short and heavy, her legs were thick and unhealthy with ulcers and blood clots. I always thought I was her

22

favorite. One day I must have said it out loud and my Mother told me in no uncertain terms that she did not like her Mother. She only liked her Father. In fact, I only saw my Mother cry once m my whole life and that is the day her Father died. My Mom told me that when my Father died her Mother told her to put us kids in an orphanage. I was pretty grown up when this happened but it bothered me so much that I never had that good feeling about her anymore - especially on the days my Mother would get mad for some reason or other and make us pack our bags and sit on the front porch waiting for the orphanage to pick us up. My Mother was a bitter, bitter woman. (By the way, it was always Mother. She never allowed us to call her Ma, Mom, etc. always Mother).

My Grandfather Kennedy was just that, my grandfather. I don't remember any warmth, nothing. I remember what he looked like, but I was married before I ever talked to him. I remember the inside of his house, the smell, and my Father's pictures there.

My Grandmother Kennedy was a nice woman. She sewed for us, every thing was too big for me, though. Marlene was a big girl and I was skinny and not only were my things always big, I still had to wear Marlene's hand-me-downs, so I would be wearing the same things forever. I use to sit on my grandparents' front porch and count the cars that would go by. Our Grandmother Kennedy would let us (Marlene and I) buy penny candy on the first day of a visit, then each day she would take the bowl down from up high in her pantry and let Marlene and I pick out a few pieces for that day. It was a special treat.

Grandmother Kennedy had a bad heart and slept alone in later years with a yard stick in bed with her. This way she could bang on the wall next to her and my Grandfather would come to see what was wrong and help. After my Father died, and after my Grandfather Kennedy sold our home (70 Hull Avenue) and we moved to Trenton, NJ our Grandmother Kennedy always tried to question Marlene and I on what our Mother was up to. I think that is the only reason she ever invited us back to Freehold. Those few years came to an end all to fast and then like always our Mother did as she damn well pleased.

In later years, my Mother told me that she used to tell Marlene and I things so we would tell our Grandmother Kennedy and get her all upset - things like Mother was going to take us kids back to Massachusetts to live and that they would never see us again.

My Mother had me write my Grandfather each summer and ask for money to send us to day camp while our Mother worked. Each summer I did and Grandfather sent us to camp and also paid for our bus passes to get there. Camp was at the old deaf school in West Trenton, so it did mean a bus ride.

Here are some other family tidbits I remember:

A. My Grandfather Wilcox died from bleeding stomach ulcers in a hospital.

B. My Grandmother Wilcox died four days after a fall. She just was sitting in bed listening to the radio (as was her habit) and peacefully went to sleep for good. I took care of her for three of the four days that she lived. I should say, young Stephen and I did. I was close to delivering Christopher when I was caring for Grandmother Wilcox. Aunt Pat Wilcox Patrillo made arrangements for a lady to come in during the day and care for Grandmom until Uncle Clem got home from work. That very night Grandmom died. When she was buried I stayed at the house and took care of all the young children in the family. I didn't mind because while Grandmom was alive I took care of her during those last days. After all, I was her favorite.

C. My Grandmother Kennedy died from a bad heart.

D. My Grandfather Kennedy died of complications of old age.

E. My Grandmother Catherine (Coyne) Kennedy had a twin sister. Her name was Mary Coyne. We (kids) were taught to call her Aunt Mame because there was already a Mary, our Daddy's sister. Aunt Mame was married to Frank Snyder. They lived in Freehold and after we moved to Trenton Aunt Mame would invite Marlene and I down to visit maybe twice a year. Marlene and I would have to take a bus to Freehold and walk to Aunt Mame's house. She was a good cook and Marlene and I loved to eat.

24

Aunt Mame also had a bad heart but as a doctor and a nurse were in the family, she was well taken care of. Then one day when Marlene and I were there, Aunt Mame was in bed sick and she showed us how she was "full of water" by pressing on her legs and moving the water away and leaving an indentation. It wasn't much later when we heard that Aunt Mame was dead and, of course, we never got to go back to her home again.

Marlene and I went back to that area of Freehold just a few years ago, but we could not find Aunt Mame's house. We were close because we could smell the Nescafé coffee in the air.

F. My Godfather was Paul Coyne. He always had a bad heart, as it ran in the Coyne family. He died early in life in the Freehold Firehouse.

G. My Godmother was my Mother's sister, Aunt Pat Wilcox (Petrillo).

I went to St. Rose of Lima School in Freehold until third grade. At that point, my Mother moved us to Trenton, NJ. I received my First Holy Communion at St. Rose of Lima. Many years later (and I mean many years later) our first grandson, Alexander James Muka was baptized in the same church that Marlene, James, Patty and I were. I remember some things about those school years in Freehold. For instance, one day my Mother made rabbit stew and I had some for lunch (we walked home for lunch and walked back to school each day). That day I ran all the way back to school because I had eaten the rabbit's leg and it helped me run even faster!

There was also one day at school when a boy's mouth was all red. It was the same day the nuns were putting glass bottles out on the ledge at school to get them cold. I remember the nuns alternating the bottles and letting the boy put his mouth on them to help him with his burning mouth. Somehow the boy had eaten hot peppers and it burned his mouth. Strange what you remember.

I don't remember ever meeting my Grandmother Wilcox's father. I know her maiden name was McCarty. That would have been my Mother's Grandfather. I never met my Great Grandmother McCarty either, as far as I can remember.

25

I do remember meeting my Grandfather Wilcox's Mother. She had cancer of the nose. That is something a kid would remember because her nose was very deformed because of operations. She lived to be very old but it was that cancer that finally took her. She lived in Massachusetts and only came to visit once every few years. Most of her children stayed in Massachusetts, too.

My Grandfather Wilcox was one of 12 children. He is the only one who had any boy children and both of his boys (Uncle Al and Uncle Clem) never had any children. Uncle Al Wilcox was still alive in 2003. He was 80). This means that the WILCOX NAME from our family will never be continued.

My Grandfather Wilcox had a heavy head of beautiful, wavy hair which was mostly gray. My Mom gave her Dad our little dog named "Doc" (because it was Dr. Carry who gave him to us). Doc lived a long time, so long in fact, it was beyond our Grandfather's life. The dog finally had to be put to sleep because he missed our Grandfather so much.

My Father was a fisherman and hunter. He had a few different boats. The most popular one was "THE MICKEY MOUSE". I remember the day he put a life preserver on Marlene and picked her up and tossed her overboard. He wasn't going to do that to me, but after he put my life preserver on, over I went. Then both Marlene and I were floating in the bay. I remember sleeping overnight on my Dad's boats, too. He had so many because my Dad's parents gave my Dad anything they could because they knew he was sick and would probably die young.

Uncle Albert Webster Wilcox, (Uncle Al) is only seven years older than Marlene.

My brother Jimmy and my sister Patty were really cute kids. My brother Jimmy was named: Martin James Kennedy. We always called him Jimmy until he got married. When my Mother signed the papers to send him off to the Air Force at 17 years old, the last thing she yelled back to him was, "By the way, your real name is Martin, not James or Jimmy."

26

Another interesting story is that Grandpa Wilcox said that we had "Indian" blood in us from Chief Sitting Bull's tribe. He said the Wilcox side of the family came over on the Mayflower and because of inter-marriage, here we were. Now, you have to remember that it could be only a story a Grandfather tells his grandchildren. I don't really know but we grew up with always believing we had Indian blood.

It was Mary Ellen Morris Wilcox's Dad who made the first "ginger snap". He was a baker. Mr. Morris was last seen on the Boston Bridge and never seen again, nor was his body ever found.

On one of our trips back to Freehold, my sisters Marlene, Patty and I went to St. Rose of Lima Catholic Church and got a copy of our Father and Mother's wedding record. It read:

October 30, 1930 - Joseph Carroll Kennedy, son of Martin James Kennedy and Katherine

Coyne Kennedy, married Marion Rita Wilcox, daughter of Albert Webster Wilcox and

Mary E. McCarty Wilcox. Ages: groom, 19 and bride, 19. Witnesses: George Conover and Katherine Ryan. John A. Kucker, Officiated.

Mother and Daddy had their wedding reception at the Battlemonument Country Club in Freehold.

Dad worked at A & M Kaiagheusian Rug Mill since the age of 17, assistant foreman to his father.

Here's another interesting tidbit, the way my Grandfather Wilcox made cough medicine. He would take clean chopsticks and lay them across a soup bowl. Then he'd carefully lay sliced onion on top. Then he poured honey over the onion slices. Time after time he would spoon up the honey and put it once again over the onion rings. I loved it but never had a cold, so I had to fake it just to get a taste.

The Wilcox family lived on Lafayette Street in Freehold. I believe that Uncle

Junior/Uncle Al was the only child born in Freehold. Marion Rita Wilcox (my mom) and her sister Eleanor were born in Lowell, Mass. Clement and Patricia were born in Amsterdam, NY.

27

I remember one day our little Patty somehow fell on a small round curtain rod and ripped through her cheek. Her little red and white dress was a mess of red by the time she got cleaned up by our Mother. Patty's side of the story is that one of her big sisters "gave" her a broken curtain rod to play with.

Aunt Pat Wilcox was engaged to George Tealy, but married Gene Petrillo instead. Aunt Pat also dated Dr. John Witman who was our boys' pediatrician in Yardley, PA.

Here's another interesting truth - Uncle Al Wilcox dated Bruce Springstein's mother. He also dated the shoemaker's daughter, Flosie Gamgimy, the prettiest girl in town. Or, so I'm told.

My baby book was given to me by Francis Gleason in March 1943. My Godfather was Paul Coyne and Godmother was Patricia Wilcox (Petrillo). I was born on February 27, 1934; seven pounds, 12 ounces at 70 Hull Avenue, Freehold NJ. Dr. Carey was the physician.

Marlene, my sister, was born on a Saturday, October 3, 1931, Dr. Carey was her physician and Beth Salman, her nurse. Godfather was Clement Wilcox and Godmother was Mary Kennedy Barlow. Marlene weighed seven and a half pounds at birth and was also born on Hull Avenue.

Martin James Kennedy, my brother, who was called "Jimmy" until he married, was born on Friday, August 7, 1936. He was born at the Freehold Hospital and weighed in at seven pounds, four ounces. Again, delivered by Dr. Carey. Paul Coyne and Patricia Wilcox were his Godparents. He was named after Grandfather Kennedy. He was also operated on for a hernia at Four months of age at Long Branch Hospital, by Dr. John Maher.

Patricia Mary Kennedy (my sister Patty) was born on January 5, 1939. It was a Thursday and Patty was born in the evening, weighing in at nine pounds and four ounces. Doctor Carey again delivered with the nurse being Aunt Mary Kennedy-Barlow. Patty was named after two Aunts, Patricia Wilcox and Mary Kennedy. Vincent Coyne and Lucille Liebler were her Godparents. Patty was born at home, like Marlene and I. Both Marlene and

I remember the night of Patty's birth. Aunt Mary brought Patty into our bedroom and said, "Here is your little sister."

My Grandpa Kennedy came from Hell's Kitchen in NY. Martin Kennedy, child of Michael Kennedy and Johanna Blood. He was born December 23, 1878 and baptized January 12, 1879 at the Church of Sacred Heart of Jesus, Borough of Manhattan. His sponsors were

Michael Kennedy and Ellen Hickey.

The Rev. Thomas J. Higgens baptized.

We were told never to buy Axminister rugs. Cheap,cheap,cheap. Of course, they are not made any more. As the story goes, a hook went thru Grandpa Wilcox's hand while at work in the rug mill. The rug mill is long gone - the building has been used by many different companies and suffered a fire a few years back.

Grandmoms Kennedy and Wilcox never worked outside the house after marriage.

Now, here's something I know as fact, when the Radio City Music Hall in New York was first built my Grandfather Kennedy (then around 68 years old) helped lay the carpet just before it opened. My Grandfather turned out to be a boss at the Kaiagheusian Rug Mill in Freehold, NJ and that is where my Father worked also. Together they invented a "cleaning process for Persian rugs." My Grandfather Wilcox also worked at the rug mill. Kaiagheusian's was a big name at the time and was the largest employer in Freehold. The rug mill was what brought my Grandfather Wilcox from Amsterdam, NY with his family to Freehold NJ because he could find work there. My Grandfather Kennedy had a laboratory down in his basement at 137 South Street, Freehold, NJ to work on new inventions.

When I was about five years old my Aunt Mary Kennedy married Dr. John Barlow. I was one of the flower girls at the wedding along with my sister, Marlene. The only thing I can remember from that day is my Aunt Mary and Uncle John took us to a candy store and bought us some sweets. Of course, I got candy stains on my pretty dress. Marlene and I also remember that when we went to Grandma Kennedy's she would always have sweet gherkins pickles for us.

Grandpa Kennedy once told Marlene, "We all have to get old someday."

When Marlene was really young she ran away quite a bit. You could not keep her in the back yard. I've heard all kinds of stories about how Mother would tie her to something, just to have her disappear. Finally, the decision was made to have a fence put up around the entire back yard. The workmen came and Marlene was spell bound. She watched the workmen the whole day long. Just as soon as they left, Marlene went over the fence and headed for the boy's academy down the street. More often than not that is where Marlene would end up. The police would call our house and say, "DO YOU KNOW WHERE MARLENE IS?" and Mother would have to bundle up us little ones and go get her. Or, if it was around the time Dad was due home from work for lunch or dinner, Mom would tell him to pick up Marlene. Remember, now, she was around four, five or six, in a small town, when this was going on.

The Applegates lived behind our home in Freehold and now there was a fence. No problem. Marlene could manage that too.

We kids had pet ducks in our back yard. Our dad always had a boat or two. Also had a car or two. He and our Mother made a stone wishing well in our back yard to match the pool.

My Mother also told me once that my toy baby carriage was imported from England and more expensive than any carriage I had for my own children. What I'm trying to say is we were one of the rich families in town.

I can remember my Daddy coming home from fishing and teaching me how to clean a fish.

I was so worried about hurting the fish. He told me that the fish were dead and they didn't hurt any more.

In thinking about him, you might imagine him a giant of a man, but years later I wore his raincoat until I outgrew it.

My Grandparents Kennedy lived two or three doors away from

30

Hulse Gas Station (you could buy penny candy there) at 137 South Street, Freehold, NJ. Hulse is no longer there.

Joseph Carroll Kennedy (my father) was born on April 2, 1911 and died on January 10, 1941 He was 29 years and 9 months old. He died in Fitkin Hospital, Neptune. His funeral was held at William H. Freeman in Freehold. When he died Marlene was 9, I was 6,

James was 4 and Patty, 2. My Dad had only one sister, Mary, and no brothers.

Dad's in-laws were Mary Wilcox and Albert Webster Wilcox. Their children were: Marion (my mom), Eleanor (my aunt), Clement (my uncle), Patricia (my aunt Pat) and Albert (my Uncle Jr.)

Dad's funeral mass was held at St. Rose of Lima's Church. Pastor at that time was Father John Kucker. Poll bearers were Jerome Coyne, Raymond Coyne, Paul Coyne (my godfather), Vincent Coyne, Elmer Archer and George Conover. Additional relatives names are Mrs. Winifred Cunningham and Joe Coyne. I think Joe Coyne was the father of the four Coyne brothers. More names from Freehold are Kathryn Barlow, Bill Madden and Ena Backalow.

When my Father died at the age of 29, the phone call came to our home and Marlene answered the phone. Our Mother called Uncle Clem Wilcox, (her brother) and he came to watch over us while my Mother went to pick up Grandpa Kennedy and Grandma Kennedy and go to the hospital.

It has been a tradition for my sister Marlene and I (and sometimes Patty) to go back to Freehold where we were born. We would go for lunch and then go visit the graves of our parents, our grandparents on both sides, aunts and uncles. There's a lot of history there.

Here I just want to say that 10 years after my Father died, my Mother remarried. She was 39 years old. She married Jeffrey A. Callahan, had a baby boy and named him Jeffrey A. Callahan. But our little brother's Dad died shortly before he was born. Our whole family is very close to our brother Jeff.

Patricia Kennedy, our baby sister was always called Patty. (When we were young, I always called her Honey, but in later years it went back to Patty). Patty is known as "PAT" to her friends and co-workers.

My Mother named me after my Father. He wanted a boy so, Carolyn Joan Kennedy was as close as he could get. (It was another two years before Jimmy was born and then he was named after Grandfather Kennedy). My Mother insisted I should be called Joan the first year of my life. That lasted until one day, however as when she was out walking me in the baby coach my Mother ran into an old school chum. Her name was Joan and she was fat, so my Mother changed me to Carolyn and informed the whole family to call me that from then on.

My Father and Mother built an in-ground pool and well to match m our back yard at Hull Avenue, Freehold, NJ. The pool was only about three feet deep, and mostly had gold fish in it, except for when Marlene and I took them out and lined them up along the sides of the pool. Even then, the gold fish were so expensive, both of us remember the spanking our Father gave us. I ran away from home, right next door to our neighbor's house.

Our Father loved animals. We had ducks, although I don't know what happened to them. And of course, the dog Penny.

I also remember that my Dad would slit the throat of the chickens and hang them up by their feet to bleed out in front of the opened garage door. We would later eat them. All this was normal because that is the way you lived in those days.

One day my Dad came home from fishing with a bucket full of crabs. They were all alive and he and Mother really laughed when Dad spilled them out on the kitchen floor and we kids screamed with delight as the crabs scrambled all over the place.

There was also a lot of canning and preserving done in those days. Our Mother made grape jelly and orange marmalade and relishes.

In Trenton, we went to Saint Anthony's Grammar School on Olden Avenue. I went from fourth to eighth grade. Our little Patty was so young when we moved to Trenton, but our Mother had to work, so Patty was sent to kindergarten a year earlier than usual. So the next year she was just the right age and had to stay in kindergarten for another year. Patty was so little that the walk from Greenwood and Connecticut was very long and hard on her, especially when it was cold out.

We ended up in Trenton because Uncle Clem was working there. Our Grandfather Kennedy was named on the deed to the house at 70 Hull Avenue. My parents were too young to own property, since they were both 19 years old when they married. When our parents moved in that house after they were married it was completely furnished, food in the ice box and pantry, sheets and blankets in the closets, etc. Our parents paid the monthly payments on the house and the mortgage was just about paid off when my Father died.

Of course, my Grandparents Kennedy did not like many of the things my Mother would do after that. My Mother told them where to go and the next thing you know, our Grandfather Kennedy had put the house up for sale. It sold, of course. My Mother's pride carried her through, but she still did it her way.

She had to sell the car, boat, diamond, Father's tools, etc. But, long before women's lib our Mother got a mortgage on a house with the help of Uncle Clem and a job with the State of New Jersey and we were living on the corner of Greenwood and Connecticut in Trenton.

Our Grandfather told the Freehold people that one day he would leave all his money to his name sake: Martin James Kennedy, "Jimmy," of course. Well, you can guess at the end of that story, Jimmy never got any money. When Grandfather died, he left each one of us grandchildren $499 so that we would not have to pay any tax on the money.

As you can see, there is a repeating pattern with my mother. But like I said, it took a lifetime to figure things out.

Our Mother put a chip on her shoulder and all her life dared any one to knock it off - any one included her own Mother, her kids, her co-workers, the church, everyone. Our Mother set herself up so she came out a martyr. It was always someone else's fault. They did her wrong. She always tried to show us the bad side of everyone, and of course we believed her. Why would you not? All I know, is that our Mother was bitterly unhappy and those who were close to her paid for it. It is a wonder that we kids turned out normal, if you can call it that.

Mother's greatest gift to us was that she forced us to stick together against her in order to survive. She raised us without a Father, and without love. None of us got into trouble, but it turned her into stone. I'm sure that in order to not be like her we kids all have erred on the other side of the coin.

I know one thing for sure, I am more like my mother than any of her other children. It is why I have stayed on top of any problems I have had. I have tried to take her good points and avoid the bad ones.

I still have a close friend from my St. Anthony's school days. Her name is Barbara Seamen Cameron Cole. I still see her and spend time with her.

Ten years after my Father died, my Mother married her boss from the state job she had. Within the first year my Mother was pregnant with my brother Jeffrey. Before my brother Jeff was born my Stepfather died of a heart attack.

It was really hard on my Mother with no money coming in except for the Social Security for us. My Mother once again turned to me.

She made me sit with her and learn all the bills, the value of everything in the house. She pounded into me that I was not to let anyone, take anything out of our home it she should die. I had to keep the house going for the young kids. She warned me that my aunts or uncles might want things and not to give them anything and not to let them take anything. It went on and on. No wonder I started getting gray hair early in life.

Mother survived the birth of her fifth child, though.

Things were really tough and Mother took Marlene out of school so she could get back to work and Marlene could watch over the new baby. Within three months, I came home from school one day after being elected vice-president of my class to find out that I was being taken out of school (at the age of 14) to take care of my baby brother Jeff. Mother had gotten Marlene a job. Marlene and

I had to go to night school for three and a half years, five nights a week in order to finish high school.

This was all done with the permission of the Board of Education. Two years later (don't ask me how) I was working for the State of New Jersey in the Inheritance Tax Department. (That is where my Mother worked and where Jeff's Dad worked). Young Jeff, (about two and a half at the time) went to nursery school. Marlene and I helped pay the cost to send him there. While working for the State, Marlene and I put our applications in at the new steel mill being built in Fairless Hills, PA. If we could get jobs there it would mean a lot more money to kick in for the Revere Avenue home. (When my Mother remarried we moved to another address, at Revere and Liberty, so everyone could start off fresh. That did not last very long with our Stepfather dying). Fairless Hills Steel Mill did call. They wanted me to come in for an interview. Mother answered the phone that day and the first thing she said was, "Carolyn has an older sister. How about her?"

Well, Marlene and I both got office jobs at the steel mill, under the condition that we both stayed in night school to get our high school diploma.

I ended up being Class President of our graduating class. I'm sure they chose me because they knew it would mean so much, being the youngest one who ever graduated from adult night school. When I registered for adult school I was 14 years old, but the person in the office taking the information said, "Oh no, we can't have that." So she wrote down that I was 18. The next year it happened again, and again, until I actually turned 18 and graduated in June 1952.

I GET A BIG KICK OUT OF KIDS TODAY. THEY THINK THEY HAVE IT TOUGH. I AM NOT TALKING ABOUT THE CHILDREN I GAVE BIRTH TO. WITH MY RECORD, I BELIEVE THEY HAD IT TOUGHER THAN I DID. BUT, AS MY MOTHER WOULD SAY, "AT LEAST THEY HAD A FATHER". No comment...

Marlene and I did stick it out and both of us graduated from Trenton Central High School on June 17, 1952. One of our classmates who graduated with us was a fellow by the name of Leonard L. Muka.

My first date with Leonard was graduation night. I married him on November 27, 1952 at the sweet age of 18.

My Mother was really angry, not because I was getting married but because of the financial and emotional support my not being in her household supplied. (I still paid my share of Jeff's nursery bill after I got married, I just didn't have to pay my room and board any more).

Without realizing it, my Mother created a very independent person in me. Much like my Mother (my Mother and Father were both 19 years old when they married), I had become my own person. I felt since Leonard was older than I, born October 17, 1923), he would be a responsible person and a good Father to any children we would have. I also felt that I would not have to be so strict with myself. I would just do what a wife and Mother had to do and LET Leonard be boss. So much of the heavy responsibility would rest on his shoulders. IT HAS BEEN A LONG LIFE.

No one in my life time has ever heard me say that any problems I ever had were because I got married when I was a teenager. Maybe I was 18, but in my mind I was 100 - really old. I have been old and a worrywart all my life. I skipped over any childhood I might have had when my Father died.

At this very moment, I am living next door to the Atlantic Ocean. It feels like that it is just where I am supposed to be, like fate has had its way. A bridge of 50 years has gone by, yet in my head I could be on my Father's boat when I look out over the ocean.

My mind has always overruled my heart - always. Some times I hate myself for it, but I will never change. Just remember the sourdough - you get a starter and then make the dough. When you take the first batch and throw it up on the bench you cut a piece off and put it in the refrigerator. The next time you make sour dough you take that piece from the refrigerator and mix it in the newest batch. Each time you save a piece of it for later.

36

Life has taught me to be like that. I have always saved a piece of Carolyn no matter who or what the occasion may be. I have never given up everything for anybody, including Mother, Father, Husband, Children or Home. I have never gotten so attached to anyone or any thing, (even this shore house) that I could not live without. The key word here being LIVE.   Inside I have always felt I was a worthwhile person. I could look at myself and like myself and stand to live with myself. I was and never will be a martyr.

MY MOTHER DIDN'T RAISE NO DUMMY!

left to right: Christopher, Stephen, Lawrence, James, Michael

LEONARD
AND CAROLYN

Married life proved to be a sobering experience. the carefree, protected Carolyn lasted about a month or two. Len was boss but I never thought for a minute that if anything happened to Leonard that I wouldn't or couldn't take care of things.

My Mother said she would not come to my wedding. Mother made statements like, "One day soon, when you come home from work, all your clothes will be ripped to threads." And, "I would not walk across the street to help you if you were dying," and so on.

It was a really hard time for me, but since I had made up my mind, I was unyielding. My Uncle Clem drove me to the church (Uncle Al was Leonard's best man). Marlene stood up for me and Len's family made Len and I breakfast. It was when I turned around to leave the alter at Immaculate Conception Church in Trenton that I saw my Mother. All the time I was up at the alter I thought my Mother was not at our wedding. What I didn't know was my Aunt Pat in New York had called my Mother to tell her that she was only embarrassing herself in the eyes of other people, which included the people she worked with at the State since they all knew me. Many of the State people were there as well as the people I worked with at the steel mill. It was unbelievable because no invitations went out and there was no reception, but there were quite a few people in church. After the wedding I had announcements made and sent them out myself just announcing that Carolyn Joan Kennedy had married Leonard L. Muka.

Before our wedding, though, there were two wedding show-ers. One by my co-workers from Fairless Steel and another by Leonard's family. My Mother was invited to both but did not come to either. At Leonard's family shower there was a token gift from my Mother, a hair brush. (Funny the things you re-member).

Len and I were married on Thanksgiving Day and went to New York until the Sunday after, returning to work on Monday. We lived in Leonard's Mother's house.

The word UNYIELDING has come up several times in my life-time, when someone wanted to describe me. Looking back on that time, Len always laughed about it, because he figured it out before I did that Mother probably thought I was going to have a baby. The joke was on her. It's a shame she could not talk to me then, because the word UNYIELDING was one of the things Len had to deal with as I was a virgin when I got married. One of Len's comments on our wedding night was, "I can't believe that your Mother let you get married and not tell you anything."

I did not want to ever go back to my Mother's house. Len made me go, though, saying "If you don't go to your Mother's one day you will blame me, so let's not start off that way."

It was never comfortable every again no matter where my Mother lived. It had been polite, but very little love. In the end, Mother and I were too much alike.

A beautiful baby girl was born October 3, 1953. Len announced, "Our Dianne is here," when he came to the side of my bed in the hospital. We had not even discussed names, but I could not call her anything else because at that moment she was Dianne. On New Year's Eve our little girl died. It turned out to be SIDS, Sudden In-fant Death Syndrome. Dianne died in her baby carriage. She never woke up from her nap. I called Len at General Motors where he worked and asked him to come home.

He said I was just a new Mother and not to "get so upset." I had to tell him over the phone that Dianne was dead and to meet me at the hospital.

Of course, from the hospital we went right to my Mother's where she proceeded to tell me how lucky I was that it was my baby who died and **not** my husband. Otherwise, I would have had to raise the baby myself. Len and I stayed at Mother's until we got the answer from the hospital on why Dianne died. SIDS, they told me over the phone, and it was not my fault. There was nothing that I could have done.

The police were waiting for us when we got back to my Mother's. A report had to be filled out because a child had died. The police had already questioned Len's family and the neighbors about what kind of Mother I was. I asked to go upstairs to go to the bathroom. Len's brother John jumped up to stop me because he thought I was going to harm myself. I had to assure him I was fine. (After all, I had seen my Mother and you better believe I was going to be OK). I was all of 19 years old.

Len's family loved me and was always very supportive of me. My Mother-in-law had all the love I was looking for. She spoke broken English but we understood each other very well, except when she would forget and just talk Slavic to me and we would both start laughing. Then she would have to start all over again. Each of us girls, Marlene, Patty and I maried into families who loved us. We all loved our Mothers-in-law and they showered their love on us. And we just ate it up. Our Mother was so tough, I know she had to be, but it was so hard thinking that she didn't love us. When your own Mother does not love you, who could love you?

The scar Dianne's death left on my sisters and me was that as each new baby was born into our families, we never felt at ease until each baby passed the three-month mark.

God was good to Leonard and me and on October 18, 1954 our first son was born, Stephen Muka. (I am so sorry I did not give my children the middle name of Kennedy). Stephen was named after Leonard's Father.

At this point, Len and I moved to Levittown, PA into a little rancher. Len's Mother called it "Little Bethlehem."

On December 26, 1956 a second son was born to us. We named him Christopher Muka. Christopher because it was so close to Christmas.

On August 25, 1959 a third son was born. We named him Michael Muka, after Father Michael Bakaisa.

On February 4, 1961 a fourth son was born. We named him Lawrence Muka. It was the closest we could come to Leonard without making Lawrence a junior. I just would not let anyone nickname him Junior like my Uncle Al, who was called, Uncle Jr.

On December 16, 1963 a fifth son was born. We named him James Muka because I always liked that name.

All of the children were born at Mercer Hospital, Bellvue Avenue, Trenton. Stephen was only a few weeks old when we moved to Levittown, PA. Even though we lived in Pennsylvania we went back to the same doctors and hospital to have all our children. IT WAS A GOOD LIFE AND ALL I EVER WANTED, our little Bethlehem.

By the way, the two years we spent with Len's Mom we paid good money for our room and board. It was a big help for Len's Mom to run her house. When we left (we had to leave because it was too hard to raise another baby in the house on Lamberton Street, Trenton, NJ). Len's Mom came to our new home and washed cabinets, dishes, etc. to help us get the house ready. Aunt Betty (Leonard's sister), had to leave her job working for Father Bakaisa and stayed with her Mother to help pay to run the Lamberton house.

Len's Mother was 72 years old when I joined the family. I was 18 and didn't know anything because I was too young (per Len's Mom), and she didn't know any better because she was too old (per Carolyn). WORKED FINE FOR ME.

While I was with my Mother-in-law waiting for two babies (Dianne and Stephen) I realized that she was not receiving Social Security. I knew all about Social Security because my family received it after my Dad died. Social Security had only been in effect for about three years when my Dad died. It helped my Mother keep us together. I was about eight months with child when I took my

Mother-in-law (who didn't speak English very well and whose birth certificate was a torn piece of brown paper that the mid-wife wrote on when my Mother-in-law was born and came from a country across the ocean), to the courthouse in downtown Trenton. I just had to see why she wasn't getting Social Security from the benefits of her late husband working in this country. (I never met my Father-in-law, he died before Len married me). In a few short months, Len's Mother was receiving a Social Security check each month. She was so happy and proud to have her very own money. When she came to visit it was always with lollipops or cookies - enough for her grandchildren and her Carolyn.

My Mother was only in my Mother-in-law's company ONCE. My Mother-in-law made the mistake of saying "MY CAROLYN" and my Mother jumped up, stood over her and said "MAKE NO MISTAKE, SHE IS NOT YOUR CAROLYN." Never again would anyone let my Mother near my Mother-in-law. It wasn't too hard to keep them apart, though. My Mother-in-law came to visit at least once a week, Aunt Betty would bring her to see the boys. My Mother would never come with out a special invitation just for her, so I always knew when she was coming. With five boys to raise it was hard to set aside special time for my Mother. My Mother-in-law was just there. She rocked the babies, folded wash, matched socks. I loved her. My Mother was a business women. You shook her hand, you didn't kiss her. (MY MOTHER DIDN'T TAKE ANY PRISONERS).

All in all things went very well. Len took a quick course in engineering at Drexel Night College that took eight years. He graduated with a degree in Mechanical Engineering.

By now my brother James, my sisters Patty and Marlene all were married. (Marlene, the oldest, was the last to get married. It took her longer to find a husband). Jeff was the last to be with Mother. That is a story in itself; he had it worse than we did in another way. Money was better, they went on vacations, he had nice cloths, got away with murder, but he was alone and Mother owned him. The four Kennedys had to stick together. Our brother Jeff had a differ-

43

ent kind of upbringing. When Mother died we were afraid for him but for years we three sisters made it a point to stay close to Jeff and it really paid off when Mom died. He had a good support system.

Like every family, it had its ups and downs, but we stuck together. This is something our Mother taught us. Mother bought the grandchildren nice gifts when she could, was interested in what they were doing from a far distance. She would never go to a game they played in, or a school function. But, get your name in the paper for something good, graduate, get an award? She was all for showing it off. Always from a distance, as she never put her hand on your shoulder, never kissed me or the boys, and never let you kiss her. She just could not make herself show any kind of love. She really believed it was a weakness if you showed any emotion. I guess I have some of that in me, but I work really hard at not being like that. Sometimes even now, though, I feel I am just too independent for my own good...

My brother Jimmy "Martin James Kennedy"
married Patricia Drew.
They had four children:
Joseph - July 16, 1960
Carol - January 14, 1962
James - August 27, 1964
Margaret - September 1, 1966

My sister Patty "Patricia Kennedy"
married George Sampson on November 26,1960.
They had three children:
Albert Webster - February 6, 1961
Marion - March 12, 1963
Suzanne - October 12, 1965

My sister Marlene "Marlene Kennedy"
married Arthur Tomczyk September 3.
They had four children:

Mary Anne - December 18, 1961
Barbara – February 8, 1964
Nancy Ann - February 27, 1966
Amy - February 24, 1972
Sixteen grandchildren in 16 years didn't make Mother happy.

From Levittown our family went to Michigan. Len was transferred to the Detroit plant. So in a four-cylinder car (I know it was because it was one of the first things that had to be changed. No one in Detroit drove a four-cylinder because speed limits were seventy miles an hour on some roads). We ended up living in a beautiful new home, again our little Bethlehem. James, the youngest, was 9 months old at that time.

The next year and a half in Michigan:

Michael had a very bad injury to his elbow. He fell off a swing in kindergarten. We were told that there was a chance that his arm would not grow from that point on, as the soft tissue in his elbow was very badly injured. Needless to say, everything turned out fine but it took a year before we got an "all clear" on that arm.

James had a hydro seal and a rupture that put him in the hospital. His operation was successful but he came home from the hospital sick. The doctors told me that James was so home sick, that even though they wanted him in the hospital a few days, he should go home with me (the day after the operation). I carried him from his hospital room all the way to the car. I wouldn't even put him down to rest. Once home he was fine.

Stephen, Christopher and a male neighbor helped Len make a cement patio in our back yard. Very nice, Len put a white picket fence around it so James would have a large play pen and could be outside with his brothers.

While Len was kneeling down he hurt his knee and it swelled up. Doctors said it had to be operated on, so Len went off to the hospital to be operated on. That operation was a success, but in the end a blood clot passed from the knee to Len's heart and caused his

45

first heart attack. The hospital was trying to teach Len how to walk with crutches when Len complained of pains in his chest. The boys and I went immediately to the hospital.

Stephen watched his four younger brothers in the hospital lobby while I went to Len. A nun came by and asked "Why are you children here?"

Stephen answered, "Our Mother went to see our Father."

"What is your Father's name?" the nun asked.

"Leonard Muka," Stephen answered.

"Oh, you poor kids," she said. "Your father is so sick. He had a heart attack. He may not live."

By the time I got back to the boys, poor Stephen was white as a ghost. I felt so sorry for Stephen. Like me, he was so grown up for his age. He was only about 11 years old but the oldest of the five boys.

Our friends from General Motors were great. They scheduled the mothers to come to our home, one each afternoon so I could go be with Len in the hospital. It was a very trying time, getting Stephen, Christopher and Michael off to school each day, Lawrence and James at home, get to church, Boy Scouts, etc. No one ever missed a step.

One afternoon when I went to leave for the hospital, our Buick station wagon had a flat tire. The lady who was babysitting said, "Take my car." It was a brand new white Cadillac. I stopped on the way home to refill the tank with gas and the station attendant could not find where to put the gas in the car, since the car was so new. I had to return it to the lady without filling the tank.

Len was in the hospital about ten days. The day I drove him home he was so upset about coming home with me, he said that they should have sent him home in an ambulance. I had gotten pretty good about keeping up with the traffic on those 70 miles per hour roads!

During this time there was a lot to take into consideration. Here we were in Michigan with no family except our own. I was told not to make a cardiac cripple out of Leonard and Leonard

46

was told not to worry about his family so much that it would give him another heart attack. Len was not himself for a long time. He wrote letters to his office at GM and told them what they were doing wrong, etc. I had to type the letters for him and told Len that he was going to end up back in Trenton working for the A&P. I wasn't that far wrong.

Len asked to go home, and we were back so fast it would make your head spin. We ended up in Yardley, PA. Shortly after returning, Len of course was given a demotion and he would not stand for that, so he quit. (Seventeen years at GM down the drain). In a few weeks we were working in OUR own bakery. So it wasn't the A&P, but close. Things have never been the same. Eight years going to school to become an engineer, just to become a baker. The whole family worked at the bakery. All this brought me to my knees.

I remember one day going to church when no one was around, walking right up to the alter and saying out loud to God, "You know what is going on. Give me the strength and I'll use it." The bakery was a part of our life that lasted about a dozen years and we still talk about it. Of course, no one wants to bake much anymore.

We lived in Yardley about 17 years. Len worked at GM, then the bakery and Revere Company. And at one point no job at all. Yardley was beautiful. The boys went to St. Ignasus School and then on to Bishop Egan High School. It really was a wonderful place to raise the boys. They should have grown up to be saints, but that didn't happen (ha ha). They did get a good education and in the end those who wanted to went to Rider College and graduated - Christopher, Lawrence and James.

LIFE HAD TAUGHT US A LOT OF LESSONS BUT THE BIGGEST LESSONS WERE YET TO COME.

TWELVE YEARS

This begins our next 12 years in "My Nieces' Bakery," Main Street, Yardley, PA.

Each boy had to work along with us. Stephen was 13 by then so he, Christopher and Michael had to help right off. Once 9, Lawrence and James both had to go to work. At first, everyone wanted to help, but as time went by we were all tired. It was especially hard on the boys because they also wanted to do scouts, basketball, etc. And as parents we wanted good grades. Being they all went to Catholic school, the same rules applied at school that applied at home and at the bakery.

I learned to decorate cakes and work the store. At least once a week I was ready to sell the business. It didn't pay us much, but I must say it kept us out of trouble since everyone was too tired. I worried a lot, thinking if anything happened to Leonard there would be no business. It was really a big chance to take. In the end it took everything we had, and we had to sell the bakery and our home in Yardley, but I'm getting ahead of myself.

Stephen got out of the bakery by going to college right out of eleventh grade. He was 16 years old and went off to "Deep Springs College" in Nevada. Christopher hung in there with us and also helped out with the Pizza Place next door to the bakery. Michael, Lawrence and James hung in there also until the bakery was sold. There were a lot of hard times, but a lot of good times, too. Our boys had a lot of friends because there were always leftovers and we shared a lot. Some of our neighbors complained when they found bags of donuts or trench bread under their kids' beds when their moms would find crumbs during her weekly cleaning.

We had an above ground pool in our backyard. But with all the work that had to be done the pool was the last to get any attention. The neighborhood kids called our pool "Muck Water." They had pools much nicer than ours, but we had the bakery leftovers every night so it got to be quite a popular place. Our social life got to be the bakery, with neighbors and friends and family always stopping in. The kids on there way home from anywhere would be there. Even our priest would stop in.

One day in the spring, a group of boys from St. Ignasus School decided to ride their bikes to school and at lunch time they took off and did not go back. The first place the school called was our bakery to see if the boys were there.

No one felt sorry for our sons, they thought how lucky the boys were that they got to play with flour and sugar, instead of dirt. Our boys worked like men plus there was always cleaning to do. One day I remember an inspector came in with a trainee.

He told the man, "I brought you here first, to show you how a back room in a bakery should look."

That made me feel pretty good. Lawrence could take a bow for that, as he kept the floor clean. It was the only job in the bakery that Len would pay to have done so Lawrence earned five bucks a week keeping it clean. Len always told the boys that their room and board and their Catholic school education was their pay. Believe me, the boys earned it.

I would always say that all my diamonds and furs were my boys. I thought all my boys would become priests and I would just go from rectory to rectory taking care to see that everything was run right. Well, that is not how it turned out. There was never much money, but somehow we made do for those dozen. No vacations, but each Labor day weekend Father Bakiasi and Aunt Betty would have us down to Lavallette (shore) and we had the greatest time. We lived in a beautiful neighborhood where all the families did a lot of things that our kids did not get to do, but in the end it help them deal with what was to come.

On Mother's Day 1975, the boys and Len bought me a beautiful second-hand car. Up to that point we only had one car and Len drove that. You could walk down town to our bakery and most times that is what I had to do. It was no problem, but on the way home it was always tough because I would have been on my feet all day. If I didn't get a ride home with Len, or for some reason he could not get back, I walked. People were used to seeing me walk back and forth.

Having a second car was a big thing, it meant I could do my share of car pooling. Plus, in Pennsylvania you cold drive at 16 years of age and the boys took advantage of that a lot.

Because the bakery would never have worked at all if it weren't for the free labor from the boys, Len was always trying to get rich quick. That is where Wilber Duncan came into the picture. Christopher ran the bakery by then and Len was off to folly with Applied Research Prducts, Davis Station Road, Creamridge, NJ. In the end, Len did not make any money and we were sued. It was a mess, but of course (as usual) it was NOT Len's fault. (A lifetime attitude that Len always had). The bakery had to go and along with it our home in Yardley.

By then, Stephen was in college. Christopher went to Parks College, Ill.My brother Jeff was working at Rider College in Lawrenceville, NJ. He kept after the boys and me, telling us that if I worked at Rider the kids could go to college for free.

Well, to make a long story short, on Mother's Day that year the boys sat me down and said they wanted me to go to work at Rider so they could go to school there. I cried myself to sleep that night as finally the bakery was sold, I had been married for over **25** years and they wanted me to go out to some strange place and go to work.

The next day called Rider, had an appointment for Tuesday and started working on Thursday. Christopher came home from Illinois. Then it took another 12 years, but Christopher, Lawrence and James all got their college educations from what is now called Rider University. Stephen went from Deep Springs to the University of Chicago. Michael was signed up, did all his pre-testing had his physical and kept begging off going to college. In the end he did not go, but that is another story in itself.

There's so much to say. I thought if I wrote it I could let it all go. But it is not working **out that way.** Maybe it is because I know what is coming up and I am not sure I want to put myself through it all over again.

Some of the best memories of the bakery were the good breakfasts that Len would make the boys in the bakery's ovens. Len would

50

take new aluminum pie pans, put a little grease on them, then liverwurst and eggs, and pop them into the oven. Everyone would have their own breakfast. All the boys drank lots of milk, especially Michael. On one particular day, Michael drank three half-gallons of milk. This is also the time and the place where the boys learned to drink coffee. To this day we are all big coffee drinkers.

The Catholic schools had to use the public school buses, so this meant our family had to be up, homework done, kids fed, lunch and books in hand, plus be dressed in trousers, white shirts, ties, and out on the corner ready to be picked up by **6:30 a.m.** This was so the buses could be available for the public school students.

With the bakery training we were always getting up really early. The whole family had a good work ethic and still get up early to this day.

The bakery had an alumni of young ladies who worked the counter. For years, the girls would come back and thank Len for their training. It helped them later in life with other jobs. You could say the same thing with our sons. All the hard work, scheduling their time, and their Catholic school education did them well later on in life. We made a lot of friends in Yardley. Everyone knew our family. One of the unforgettable ones was Catherine Welsh.

Our bakery was called "My Niece's Bakery" because my Uncle Al was a milkman who delivered in Yardley. On his route he told his customers that his niece bought a bakery. Each day he would ask them if they had tried his niece's bakery. A lot of people came in because of Uncle Al. One poor soul asked me for a pencil and a piece of paper. Please give your Uncle my name and tell him I came in. It was so funny that we changed our bakery's name from Kay's to "My Niece's Bakery."

When we sold our bakery, another baker bought it. There was a news article in the local paper: which said "Mr. and Mrs. Charles Rudnik of Trenton have purchased 'My Niece's Bakery' in Yardley from Mr. and Mrs. Leonard Muka who have operated the bakery for many years in the shopping center. The Rudniks will rename the bakery 'Hermitage Pastry Shop.'"

51

Really, it was an education in itself. Never buy a bakery, though. It is harder than the White House. Our bakery was sold on January 29, 1978.

We always followed the boys playing basketball. They all played, but the closest we came to having a superstar was James. Years later, after they were all grown up, one of the boys asked me, "Mom, how come we only ever played basketball?"

My answer was, "It was the only sport I liked." After all, I did birth my own basketball teams with five boys!

Just for the record: Len worked at Mercer Rubber Company, 136 Mercer Street, Trenton after Applied Research and after we sold the bakery in 1978.

When I started working at Rider College , it was in the bookstore. Again, I made a lot of friends, some who have lasted a lifetime. While there, Len and I hosted a dinner in our Yardley home for the whole bookstore group. It proved to be a wonderful time that night.

Having boys, it sometimes was hard. They were young and strong and would try anything. I have to say that one day when James was young, and about to go to high school, he was at the age when I knew there would be drinking at parties. I asked him if he had ever had a drink of alcohol and he said no, but he would like to try. I opened the closet door and told him to help himself. I told him to try all the different drinks and see what he thought. Well, he thought that was great. A couple of hours later he was very sick, throwing up and everything. He was really mad at me, but he **NEVER** seemed to have a problem with friends and drinking. He knew what would happen and handled himself very well. (After all, if you can't trust your own Mother, how can you trust your friends when it comes to drinking).

The Yardley house was on a large corner lot. We did a lot of living in that house. We lived longer in that house than we lived any other place in our married life. It was a big house and there was no problem having enough room for our family.

While at Rider I took two college classes. In the first one I got a B and in the second one I got a C, so I didn't go anymore. I really didn't like going to school at night after work. As I sat in the classes it reminded me too much of the three and a half years of going to night school for my high school education. I really didn't want to do that all over again in 1982. I was already 48 by then.

I enjoyed Rider's Athletic Department, though. Alter working in the college store for three years I transferred to the athletic department. It was a lot of hard work, but it also brought me more in touch with the young students, and I liked that. Following their sports proved to bea great time for me.

EIGHTEEN YEARS

A lot happened within the next 18 years. I will try and condense it and explain the best I can later.

In 1979 Stephen was diagnosed with Hodgkin's Disease (cancer) in Chicago. It took the next five years and a lot of treatments to get to a point where the doctors said that Stephen was cured. Shortly after that, Stephen came down with a childhood disease that many children get and get over with out any trouble, but because Stephen's autoimmune system was shot from the Hodgkin's and all the treatments, he became dangerously sick. In order to keep him alive he was given hundreds of bags of platelets and pints of blood. In the end, the doctors saved Stephen's life, but had given him AIDS. Stephen died one year later. He was 30. This was July,11, 1985.

(By this time, Leonard and I had sold our house in Yardley and moved into a second floor apartment in Ewing, Trenton, NJ).

On July 22, 1985 (11 days after Stephen died), Michael was hit by a drunk driver and left a quadriplegic. Once again, we were by the side of another son in the hospital. Michael lived nine years this way and died December 5, 1994.

The day after Thanksgiving, 1986, Christopher's van was hit head on by a young, underage, drug addict in a stolen car. Christopher was left in a coma with his right side broken up. He suffered a head injury that left some residue, but what he is today is great, but you have to understand that's after many years.

53

In 16 months, one son died after a six-year struggle, one son was a quad and in a nursing home and one son was hanging on to life in a coma.

In May 1987, Christopher finally got home from the hospital, (To our second-floor apartment). October of that year Leonard also had a triple by-pass surgery for his heart. In November of 1989 I had a serious back operation.

Some where through these times, Lawrence and Malou got married and brought Malou's daughter "Faye" here from the Philippines, had a baby girl named Kimberly, and shortly after that Lawrence and Malou divorced. James and Magda were married. A year later Lawrence met Laura and they married. Somehow, Christopher, Lawrence and James went to and graduated from Rider College, now a University in Lawrenceville, NJ.

In 1993 Len's sister "Aunt Betty," (who lived with us) died from cancer. My Michael died in 1994 and in 1995 my Mother died. In 1997 Dick Daly died.

Well, 1996 was a good year.

STEPHEN

BE YOURSELF
(I don't know who wrote it)

The world would like to change you, there are pressures all around.
You must decide just who you are, then firmly hold your ground.

You have an image of yourself, an ideal sense of you. And to this vision you must always struggle to be true.

You know what you are good at, and you know where talents lie. But if you're ruled by others, your uniqueness could pass by.

Remember, there is much to learn, but all new things aren't good. Wisdom lies in what you've learned and what you have withstood.

So, be yourself and don't allow the world to take control. Preserving your identity is life's most precious goal.

THE LIFE STORY OF STEPHEN L. MUKA
(WRITTEN BY HIS FATHER)

The sixteen-year-old junior in high school received three awards: Math, English, Stats. 1530 Accepted in Deep Springs. Never finished high school. Left home at 16 to go to two-year college where between 20-25 students were taught by educators who were on sabbatical (usually to write a book). This was a ranch with all the work done by students. Never did finish. After a year and a half he took off and went to Idaho to live with Julie Peterson, the sister of another student. Julie had a job teaching. Another year went by and Stephen enrolled in Chicago University. While on a work-study program he wrote a computer program for Dr. Kaye, a psychologist. He met Ann Wells there. This after plans to marry Julie came to a sudden stop after the wedding cake was already baked. (They wanted children and could not afford them, so why marry?) Stephen joined a computer club – five members started US Robotics.

When push came to shove, two members dropped out, leaving Steve (by now he changed the spelling of his name), Paul and Casey. Casey's dad helped with money. Stephen lived in a one-room apartment walk-up that didn't even have a lock on the door. When we asked if he was afraid someone would rob him, his reply was no one would want what he had.

PERHAPS THE CHRONOLOGY OF THIS STORY ISN'T EXACT, BUT VERY BASIC. ONE TIME WHEN HE WAS BROKE HE CAME HOME AND WORKED IN THE BAKERY = $100 A WEEK. HE LEFT AFTER EIGHT WEEKS WITH $800.

Back to Chicago. That's when he went to Chicago University. It was after he broke off with Julie that he lived in the one-room in the integrated neighborhood. He integrated it as he was the only white person. The people of the neighborhood were very nice to him. He lived like a church mouse with not much food or clothing. Every penny he could muster went into US Robotics. He bought a used teletype machine for $300, hooked his phone up to it and accessed the computer at Chicago U. He worked on the program for Doctor Kaye from his apartment many days… **(Len didn't write any more).**

Stephen was very smart. He and Dr. Kaye worked together on a computer language called

"CRESCAT' FORTRAM-COBEL" I believe.

Alter Stephen and his partners got US Robotics off the ground (this took a couple of years) and things were already getting really good, this is when Stephen came down with Hodgkins. Stephen had many good, smart friends in Chicago, very supportive. He was already a millionaire. He researched his illness like a business problem. Deciding to go to Michael Reese Hospital and have the University Hospital of Chicago double check everything.

THINKING ABOUT THE UNTHINKABLE

This was the title of an article written about Stephen. He was at that 5-year period and considered cured. Stephen had surgery, radiation and chemotherapy. It was right after this article appeared in the Financial Statement of Michael Reese Hospital, in Chicago, as a cancer cure, that Stephen was once again in that hospital fighting for his life.

UNTHINKABLE

That is when, the childhood disease and blood/blood products came into the picture, June 1984.

Stephen had written a letter to Christopher asking him to come to work for Stephen in Chicago after graduating from Rider. Christopher did not even go to graduation when he was done. Nor was he there for his awards. He was already in Chicago working for his brother Stephen

To: Chris Muka
Dear Christopher,

This is a letter of intent concerning your involvement in two projects: The Business News Radio station idea, and the Key Board Dot.
The exact form of the corporate entity which may tackle these ideas is changing from day to day. Percentages are varying, etc...But it is my intention that you will have a significant equity interest in those ventures and at the end of a year be worth at least $1,000,000. Out of this, hopefully more.

Even if all else fails, and US Robotics elects not to give you a lot of stock in the new subsidiary, I will personally give you $1,000,000 worth of my USR stock, provided you work reasonably hard and smart at things in the next year.

Good Luck!
(Signed) Stephen Muka
7/25/84

P.S. We have also agreed to a salary of $22,000 per year.

US Robotics Inc., 477 East Butterfield Road, Lombard, Ill. 60148

Stephen and Christopher did get a Radio Magazine off the ground, but with Stephen's death things came to a grinding halt. Stephen's lawyer asked me, "Oh, Mrs. Muka, how can I help you now that Stephen is gone?"

My answer was, "Please watch over Christopher and help keep this magazine going. That is what Stephen wanted."

WELL, another long story, but in the end I got Christopher a lawyer in Chicago, held up Stephen's estate for six years but did get Christopher $850,000 of that $1 million. During that six years Christopher was badly hurt and that money made a big difference.

One day, during his last stay at the hospital, Stephen spread his charge cards out in front of me and said, "Here Mom, take these and go downtown Chicago and buy anything you want."
I said, "Stephen, I would have to carry everything back East. The only thing small enough would be diamonds."

He said, "Go ahead."

I knew he was sick then, and of course I didn't do it.

When Stephen was very sick he had two plans. Plan A and Plan B. We would talk and on his good days it was always about Plan A: He would buy new computers and stock over the phone. Plan B was if he died and what I should do.

On Stephen's last Mother's Day he and Wendy came to visit. Stephen went around to see all the relatives. Aunt Betty took me aside and said to me, "Carolyn, you are saying Stephen is so sick. He looks great to me." That was May. By July he was dead. Stephen had come to say goodbye to everyone and they didn't want to believe it.

As you may know, I am turning the pages of my scrapbooks and commenting on the things I see. I am now in Scrap Book No. 7 and just came across a suicide note that Stephen wrote. It was the night he was taken to a small hospital and then transferred to Michael Reese hospital, only this time he never came back. He died at Michael Reese a month later from

AIDS.

Dear loved ones & friends:

I love you all but feel pretty bad about myself and think we'd be better off w/o me. I'm too dangerous. Feel like a crocodile. Please don't take it too personally. Know I've left things a mess. Good luck. Love, Steve. I'm sorry.

STEPHEN MUKA, 30, FOUNDED CHICAGO ROBOTICS COMPANY

CHICAGO - **Stephen L. Muka, 30, of Downers Grove, Ill., died Thursday in the Michael Reese Medical Center, Chicago. (Thursday, July 11, 1985).**

Born in Trenton, Mr. Muka lived m Yardley, PA., and attended St. Ignatius Grammar School and Bishop Egan High School. He was a graduate of the University of Chicago, where he majored in decision sciences and computers.

He was the founger and chief executive officer of US Robotics Inc., Chicago, a firm that specialized in the

research and development of software for technical innovations, and he was a member of numerous professional organizations within his specialty.

Surviving are his parents, Leonard L. and Carolyn Kennedy Muka of West Trenton; four brothers, Christopher Muka of Chicago, Michael Muka of Bucks County, PA., Lawrence Muka of Morrisville, PA and James Muka of West Trenton; his maternal grandmother, Marion K. Callahan of Beverly; a niece and several aunts, uncles, and cousins.

A mass of Christian Burial will be celebrated at 11 a.m. Tuesday in SS. Peter and Paul Roman Catholic Church, Second and Cass Streets, Trenton. Burial will be in the parish cemetery. Friends may call Tuesday from 10 a.m. until time of the service at the church.

Memorial contributions may be made to the Michael Reese Medical Center, c/o Dr. Shapiro, Sixth Floor Unit, Lakeshore Drive at 31st Street, Chicago, Ill 60616. Arrangements are under the direction of the Saul Memorial Home, 1740 Greenwood Ave., Trenton, NJ.

July 16, 1985 was the day we buried Stephen. True to Muka tradition, Leonard, Christopher and James went out that afternoon and played golf. Unlike tradition, James and Christopher both beat their Dad in golf.

It took until July 1991 for Stephen's estate to be settled, but in the end the executor Marc J. Lane finally had to write the checks and be done with it. Remember, Stephen died in 1985.

We had good dinners and good times but the bad times overshadowed everything. We were living in the apartment when Stephen died, when Michael was hurt, when Christopher was hurt, (all in 16 monhts). It was UNBELIEVABLE, but it was one day at a time.

James and Magda got their first apartment to make room for Christopher to come home with his Mom and Dad and have the next four and a half years to get back to the point where he could take care of himself. It was a long road. Glad we didn't know what was in our future. You don't realize that is one of God's gifts until you have passed the rough spots.

On Sunday, May 11, 1986 "MOTHER'S DAY," The Times of Trenton, NJ printed an article: *Two mothers share their special stories. One is well known – a television anchorwoman; the other is known only to her family - a woman who has faced the tragedy of losing a son, and then having another left a quadriplegic by a drunken driver.*

CAROLYN MUKA

'GOD REALLY JUST LOANS YOU YOUR CHILDREN'

By Robin Lichtenstein

WEST TRENTON- It is a month forever engraved on Carolyn Muka's soul.

Eleven days after the oldest of her five sons died, her middle child became a quadriplegic when he was struck by a car as he walked home from work.

Today is the first Mother's Day since the tragedies July 11 and 22, 1985. In the wake of seemingly intolerable grief, Carolyn Muka goes on.

The stunning, strongly religious 52-year-old Rider College secretary does it by embracing a concept of motherhood she learned at age 19. Little more than a year after she married, her first child, Diane, mysteriously stopped breathing during a nap and died of Sudden Infant Death Syndrome (SIDS). She was three months old.

"Your child is God's child," Muka said recently when asked what, if any, sense has emerged from the chaos. "God really just loans you your children."

After Diane died, a doctor told Muka and her husband, Leonard, to have another baby right away. Parents of SIDS victims who hesitate through fear of it happening again risk losing

61

the courage to ever have more children, the doctor had told the young couple.

By the time she was 30, Muka had five healthy sons. With distinctly different personalities and good looks, Stephen, Christopher, Michael, Lawrence and James were destined to walk radically different paths through life.

Stephen, Muka said, was the most intelligent, ambitious and shrewd of the lot. With an I.Q. of *145*, he was accepted to Deep Springs College in Deep Springs, Calif., an institution for "only the top brains in the country," she said proudly.

After Deep Springs, Stephen continued his education at the University of Chicago. In 1978, he and some buddies from the University computer club founded U.S. Robotics in Chicago. Within three years, the company had grown into a multimillion-dollar enterprise.

"He was not perfect," the mother said stoically. "He was arrogant and ruthless. But he was very special."

While shaving one Friday morning in fall 1980, Stephen, then 25 noticed a "sizeable" lump on his neck, Muka recalled. By the time he telephoned his parents on Sunday, he already had been diagnosed with Hodgkin's disease, a potentially fatal cancer of the lymph system. He underwent the most rigorous, painful and effective treatment available _chemotherapy using some experimental drugs combined with radiation therapy.

Doctors could not explain why Stephen got Hodgkin's disease and could not say whether his brothers were at risk. To date, none of the surviving Muka brothers have been stricken.

During the first six months of treatment, Stephen was a "trooper," Muka said. After that, he began seeing Chicago psychiatrist Marc Slutsky, who helped him cope until the end.

"He was a brilliant, very talented, very creative guy who was psychologically overwhelmed by a very debilitating physical disease," Slutsky said in a telephone interview.

"He was a fighter who took values very seriously and tried to integrate them into his life."

Eighteen months after his diagnosis, Stephen was in remission, building his business and founding a publication called Radio Guide, a listing of radio station programming in the Chicago area. He turned the Guide over to Christopher, the next oldest brother, who moved to Chicago to be close to Stephen.

The following three and a half years were "very encouraging and productive," Muka said. "But in July 1984 something went terrible wrong."

Suddenly, Stephen began bleeding uncontrollably. Doctors blamed complications from the chemotherapy which severely weakened his immune response system.

"Stephen got platelets from over 300 pints of blood," said the mother who with her husband, resumed the frequent, emotionally charged sojourns to Chicago.

Despite all medical efforts, Stephen continued to weaken as hepatitis set in. Nonetheless, last Mother's Day Stephen surprised his family with a visit. Muka says she knows in her heart that he actually returned to say goodbye.

The parents stayed with their son in the hospital almost continuously during his last two weeks of life. He was lucid until suffering a stroke three days before his death. He was 30 years old. His estate was valued at $3.1 million.

Six days after the Mukas buried Stephen's ashes near the grave of their infant daughter, Michael Muka, 26, was walking home from his job at a Lahaska, PA., restaurant near Peddler's Village.

It was about 1 a.m. when a 25-year-old drunken driver plowed into a telephone pole and into Michael.

At 6 feet, 9 inches tall, Michael, the recluse of the family, towered over his brothers. His priority was to "travel and see the world," his mother said, adding it's fortunate Michael had fulfilled that dream before the accident.

Since the accident, Michael has suffered three bouts with pneumonia, a blood clot, an operation to rebuild his spine with a piece of his hip bone and bed sores "so bad that he needed plastic surgery," Muka said.

Today, he lives in a Hatboro, PA., nursing home. Empathizing strongly with his peer who caused the accident, Michael has requested that the driver be punished, but not be jailed. Michael's reasoning: Serving time in prison would change nothing and harm the man's rehabilitation rather than help it.

Muka said Michael plans to pool resources with three other quadriplegics to buy a home and 24 hour nursing care to allow them as much independence as possible. "For the first time in his life," she said, "he's thinking beyond himself."

Despite being engulfed by grief, Carolyn Muka also has thought - and acted - beyond herself: Noting the guilt and pain the drunken driver's mother must be enduring, Muka said she plans to call her to express sympathy as soon as legal action is complete. After learning of an area high school girl who broke her neck after falling off a balance beam recently, Muka called the family to offer solace.

Last Christmas, Muka decorated a Christmas tree with mirrors so Michael could see around his room even though his head was immobilized. And she made a birthday party for her newly adopted granddaughter, Feather, in January. Doing normal things, she said, helps her overcome grief. Several months ago, Muka returned to work. She takes vitamins and exercises regularly.

She said she draws strength from her family and friends, especially from her 75-year-old mother, Marian Callahan of Burlington. Twice widowed, Callahan raised five children single-handedly.

Muka keeps detailed scrapbooks on each of her son's lives. Stephen is crammed with citations for academic excellence, pamphlets from his business, ticket stubs, a lock of his wavy brown hair and photographs illustrating an unusually full life.

Turning the final page after reveling in memories of her first-born son, Muka gasped. Pasted on the page was a piece of lined paper with the letter **I** scrawled over and over. After his stroke, it was all the once-brilliant businessman could write.

"We showed it to the psychiatrist," Muka said, successfully fighting back tears. "He said it means, 'I love you.'"

CHRISTOPHER

CHICAGO RADIO GUIDE

Dear Subscriber:

No doubt you've notice that the August issue of CHICAGO RADIO GUIDE is later than normal. We appreciate your patience up to now in receiving the Guide a little late in the month. As a new publication, we've had our fair share of problems in coordinating the Post Office, Mailhouses (the people that put your magazine in the mail for us). The Printer and Radio Stations.

Unfortunately, we've encountered other difficulties that are to a certain extent out of our hands. Recently one of our co-founders passed away, Stephen Muka, a vital force to the magazine, as well as major financial contributor. His sudden and unexpected death has made Radio Guide Inc.'s major new partner the Probate Court of DePage County.

The funds which were producing CHICAGO RADIO GUIDE (like any new magazine, operating well in the red) are now going to be funneled through the courts. With two government agencies involved in production and distribution of CRG - the Courts and Post Office - there are problems even "Murphy" couldn't have foreseen.

We're asking you to bear with us while we overcome this new set of obstacles. It appears at this point that the August issue will not be published and that September will be considerably late, BUT THE CRG STAFF IS COMMITTED TO ITS PUBLICATION. Your subscription will be extended two months to make up for the lost August issue and any inconvenience we may have caused.

We at CHICAGO RADIO GUIDE hope that you take this like a champ. It really is exciting to sit back and watch the evolution of what will someday be a great magazine. Save those first issues and this letter; someday both will be worth money.

If all else fails, Radio Guide will be happy to refund the unused portion of your subscription.

Thanks for your patience and concern.

Signed Christopher Muka
Christopher Muka Development Group,
LLC Publisher

November 27, 1986 was Thanksgiving day. Christopher had been back from Chicago a few weeks and there was dinner at Barbara and Christopher's place. The next day:

TWO-CAR COLLISION LEAVES THREE INJURED IN PA

LOWER MAKEFIELD, PA – Three people were seriously injured in a two-car accident yesterday at the intersection of Edgewood and Makefield Avenues, police said. One of the drivers, Christopher Muka, 29, and his passenger, Barbara Daly, 43, both of Yardley, were listed in critical condition last night in the intensive care unit of Delaware Valley Medical Center, according to a hospital spokeswoman. Lisa Hurley, 17, of Levittown, PA., the driver of the second car, was listed in guarded condition at the medical center, a spokeswoman said. According to Sgt. Richard Scherfel, the cars coffided at the intersection, injuring all three people.

No one else was involved in the collision, Scherfel said, adding that the investigation is continuing. Scherfel said no other information was available yesterday.

Our little Kimberly was born November 19, 1986— everyone loved Kimberly, it was the first time in a very long time that our family had a new little baby. It was Kimberly's first outing, at Barbara and Christopher's. From that dinner, Len and I went straight to Michael's with his homemade Thanksgiving dinner.

When Christopher got hurt it was Magda who received the phone messages, (in our apartment in Ewing, NJ where she and James were living with Len and I). It was Magda who had to tell Leonard, James, Lawrence, Michael, Grandmom Callahan and I. Our poor Magda. She was there for James when Stephen died, she was there for us when Michael was hurt and now this, she grew up really fast being in this family.

Christopher was badly hurt, in a coma, rod in his head to read the pressure, right side all busted up. He was in and out of the coma for four weeks. This accident affected each one of us differently. It almost sent us over the edge. Christopher went straight to Magee Rehab in Philly, in the head injury department, as soon as we could get him there. I felt it was Christopher's only hope to come back to us.

One doctor told me (after Christopher was at Magee a week or two) that there was no hope for Christopher because when he came to the point he realized what had happened to his brother Stephen and his brother Michael, we would lose Christopher mentally because he would never have the will to live.

WELL, YOU DON'T TELL CHRISTOPHER'S MOTHER THAT because from then on Leonard and I got in all sorts of trouble getting Christopher up and out of his bed, untying his hands, getting his brother James to put his arms under Christopher's arm pits and holding Christopher up to a mirror. We were all screaming "You will NOT be like your brothers. You will live, you will walk again. I brought Christopher's scrapbooks into him and over and over we went through them, telling him his history but always ending up with THERE IS NO SANTA CLAUS AND YOU WILL NOT BE LIKE YOUR BROTHERS. YOU WILL LIVE, YOU WILL WALK.

There were all sorts of signs above Christopher's bed. Things such as:

THE FAMTLY IS NOT TO TAKE CHRISTOPHER
OUT OF HIS BED.

THE FAMILY IS NOT TO TAKE OFF
CHRISTOPHER'S GLOVE

THE FAMILY IS NOT TO TAKE CHRISTOPHER
OUT OF HIS WHEELCHAIR ...IS NOT, IS NOT, IS NOT

You have to realize that while all this was going on, Christopher was out of his coma but unresponsive. With the head injury, Christopher just didn't know that he was supposed to let us know he could hear us.

WELL, while at work I got an idea. I wondered if Christopher would respond to a whistle. A friend of mine at work got me a bunch of whistles (from the Rider College Security Department), and I brought them to Magee that night. Low and behold, when I blew the whistle Christopher turned. When I put the whistle in Christopher's mouth he blew it. When I asked him to blow it twice if he knew I was his Mother, he blew it twice. We went nuts. Three times for Dad. With that, the Magee forces were down the hall wanting to know what the hell was going on. I said , "Watch this. Christopher, blow it once if you know this is your nurse." One blow.

I wouldn't be surprised if they're not using that method in Magee now.

Christopher ended up coming home after one month in Delaware Valley Medical Center, Langhorne, PA and four months in Magee Rehab, Philadelphia, PA. He by-passed the nursing home where Michael was because he had a good, strong left side so he could help us when he was to be moved from a wheelchair, etc., then on to a walker, then a cane. All this took a long time but in the end Christopher walks. But to this day it is with a cane. He speaks with a horse whisper and sometimes has a short term memory problem, due to the head injury.

With a three wheel bike, Christopher learned how to get around a little bit. Len and I would stand at different corners and watch Christopher ride the bike and we would direct him back to the house. (By now we were living at 470 Miller Avenue, Trenton, NJ in a Cape Cod type house). It didn't take long before Christopher took off and we needed a car to find him. Remember, he was in his 30s riding a huge three-wheel bike.

About this time, we also had another addition to the family, Tiger, Christopher's cat. In the beginning it was to teach Christopher how to take care of someone else, but I guess he learned his lesson well.

Another lesson was the camera. A telescope was added and Christopher got beautiful with it. Also, his work on the computer was better and better. On July 10, 1988 Christopher wrote this:

HUMANS ARE A PRETTY ODD BUNCH

*They are so busy building that they hardly
notice the mutual destruction they wreck
on one another.*

RACISM ISN'T AN ORPHAN, ITS MOTHER IS SOCIETY

—clm

In September 1987 Leonard had a heart attack and ended up with a triple-by-pass. We were living at 470 Miller Avenue, Trenton, NJ. I had gotten back to work with the help of St. Lawrence Rehab in Lawrenceville, NJ, right down the street from Rider College. I would take Christopher there early in the morning, go to Rider and work, be back at St. Lawrence to pick up Christopher and bring him home on my lunch hour. At home an aid would met me and take care of Christopher for the afternoon until Len got home from his sales job on the road. That didn't work very long. I came home one day at lunch time with Christopher and found Len at the back door saying, "I need some of your Nitro." I, of course, asked why and he said "I have pains in my chest."

The aid was not there yet, so I got Christopher in the house, sat him on the couch, called our friend Richard F. Daly and said, "I am leaving Christopher with the door unlocked. The aid is not here yet, please come over and take care of Christopher until the aid arrives because I have to get Len to the hospital."

Len was admitted into Mercer Hospital in Trenton, NJ. It was his heart. I returned home to take care of Christopher, but the aid would not leave. She was afraid because she knew the history of the family. Christopher had to be taken care of and now Len was in the hospital. I told her to go, and she still would not. She went about starting tea, etc. I had a tough time getting her to believe I was OK. She went back to the office finally and wrote a report on the whole thing. She also was there for me the next afternoon when I came home once again with Christopher on my lunch hour.

After a few days in Mercer Hospital, Leonard was shipped by ambulance to Graduate Hospital in Philadelphia for a triple by-pass. Our friends took turns driving me to the hospital in Philly to be with Leonard. James and Magda brought Leonard home 10 days later. All sorts of people were called into play during the operation so that our family could be there for Leonard. Michael was kept informed by phone and Christopher had someone at home for him. Everyone did well, but we had a lot of help.

Once home, Len at first was very difficult. HE WAS GOING TO TAKE CARE OF HIMSELF AND HE WAS GOING TO TAKE CARE OF CHRISTOPHER AND THERE WASN'T GOING TO BE ANY AID AROUND etc. etc. I was a wreck. There was nothing to do but lay down the law with Leonard and in time he got to be good friends with the aid. In the meantime, St. Lawrence Rehab and Magee Rehab had been working with the Insurance Company and finally got permission to take Christopher ALL day. That was great. So instead of going home at lunch time, I started going to St. Lawrence to feed Christopher lunch. I was told in no uncertain terms that they would have none of that, that this whole thing was set up so it would be easier on me and I was to just worry about my job and they would take care of Christopher and teach him to care for himself. Christopher was there as a day patient for TWO years. He learned everyday. It was wonderful for me.

Then one day, I was told to stay awhile at St. Lawrence, they wanted a meeting with me. At this meeting, I was told that Christopher had PLATEAUED and this was it for him. It was - take him home and good luck. I had to go to work that morning and when I picked up Christopher that night he would not be going back. That was bad enough, but the fact that St. Lawrence had no hope of Christopher getting any better just blew my mind. It was the first time that Rider College had ever seen me cry. I really was upset and then got mad... You should never make me mad. I'm Irish and when I get mad I get even. It may take me a long time, but you can count on it. I do get even. As I said before, "My Mother didn't raise no dummy."

I sat down on the back steps outside our home and read all the literature I could get my hands on about what I could do for a brain injury after the institutions were done. And I want you to know that is the end of the brochures, books, etc. It stops there. When the patient is discharged, God Bless You.

Before Christopher's accident (which wasn't his fault) Christopher had graduated from Rider with honors. After the accident and after St. Lawrence Rehab, Christopher got his Master's from Rider University, and put in one year at Arkansas University on his Doctorate. I REST MY CASE.

Three years in Rider College store, eight years in Rider's Athletic Department and two years in Student Activities. All three of my sons who went to Rider had their degree so I retired to keep up with my duties at home. By then we had a grandson, Alexander James Muka and I chose to stay home and take care of him for his first year. I still had Michael, but by now he was close to us with 24-hour care in Michael's own condo. Christopher stayed with Len and I for four and a half years before we could get him out on his own again.

71

By then he could drive, shop, cook, handle his finances, etc. - all the things you needed to do to take care of yourself.

When Christopher first started to drive after his accident, (after taking the State driving course to get his license back after the head injury), he bought a van so he could just back up to the driver's seat and sit down, then bring his legs into the van. In 1995 he was doing so much better he traded in his van and bought a beautiful black Nisson.

Christopher belonged to the Walnut Street Theatre in Philly and every so often he would take me to one of the shows. (But mostly it was a great place to take girls out on a date. Christopher had it down pat).

When Christopher got out on his own, it was November 1992. It was a brand new condo, brand new furniture, etc. Magda picked out all the colors, plus appliances, rug, furniture. Len and I had our input and we set everything up so Christopher knew where everything was. There were no steps, no little lamps that he would not have been able to put on, every thing was connected so one switch on the wall in each room would turned things on - or it had it's own remote control. No dresser drawers to pull out because with one good hand and one poor hand Christopher could not pull the drawer out straight. Everything was set for Christopher to be able to manage. It didn't take long and it was old hat for Christopher. He was driving by then and that just meant he could get lost faster. He was always calling and asking how to get here or there or just how to get back home. We don't hear much of that anymore.

Christmas came that year and it was Christopher's turn to have Christmas dinner at his home. The two beautiful daughters-in-law wore their full length capes (which I had made for them) and it made me very happy. The fire was going, tree up, and food ready with the help of me. Alexander came in like he own the place, as he had been there so many times with me.

Christopher saw Spring 1993 all around him in the new condo. His home was in a corner and all you could see were beautiful woods, a lake with a fountain in the middle and if you looked real hard, deer, birds, etc. from the window. With his camera, Christopher got a lot of pictures and over time you could see the way everything filled in.

Like I said before, Christopher was his own best friend and he never said NO to me. We did, did, did. With a great deal of help from one of his old teachers, Christopher started taking classes at Rider, simple at first (remember he was an honors graduate from Rider before his accident). Later, and of course much later, Christopher wanted to enroll in the Master's Program at Rider. He asked me to find out, get the papers, etc. and I was told again in no uncertain terms that with the Master's Program at Rider, they don't deal with the parents. At that point, I let go and Christopher did every thing on his own.

A full front page in the Times newspaper had a color picture of him with his cane, receiving his master's degree entitled, "A GRAD AGAINST ALL ODDS." It was June 23, 1996.

In the Times' story and many others to follow, you will not find any credit going to St. Lawrence Rehab. I wonder how many poor souls are out there, their parents and family believing that when the institution is done with their loved one, there is nothing more to do.

We had a wonderful day when Christopher received his Master's. The next Friday night we surprised Christopher and had a family dinner at Calla's. Our family included Christopher's regular Friday night friends. I think it was the first time that Eliot was ever at a bar. (Eliot, our second grand son, 6 months old).

DELAWARE VALLEY MEDICAL CENTER
LANGHORNE, PA 12/6/96

Dear_____

Carolyn Muka will never forget the day her son, Christopher was brought to Delaware Valley Medical Center's emergency room. He was comatose, with multiple limb fractures and severe head injuries. She credits the initial care her son received at Delaware Valley Medical Center to his miraculous recovery. Numerous judgment calls by the medical staff not only saved Christopher's life, but gave him a second chance at life. Today at age 39, Christopher is a successful businessman.

Delaware etc. etc._____

(A fundraiser letter was sent out to thousands of people in the local area, asking for contributions. Christopher and I did a program for the doctors there, explaining how grateful we were for his care there and we supported their plan to use Christopher in this fund raiser.)

Christopher once sent a Christmas card to Len and I: "Merry Christmas, Mom and Dad, and Thanks. I realize it wasn't easy raising me."   and then he wrote "TWICE."

God, I must be nuts. In my scrapbook I even have pictures of Christopher's head front and back because I liked his new hair cut. Also, I have pictures of a trip which Leonard, Christopher and I took (during Christopher's recovery) to Cape May, NJ to see the Herring Nesting Area. Again, Christopher had his camera and put it to good use.

A while after the Master's degree, Christopher rented his condo in Lawrenceville and moved to a condo in Arkansas. He started to get his Doctorate at the University of Arkansas. He put one year of straight studying into it and did very well. At that point, Len and I helped Christopher make the decision to come back home. We are such a close family I think it was extra hard on Christopher to be so far away.

Anyhow, he did come back and we were so glad. Christopher, of course, grew a beard, looked like hell, and just had to come home to visit that first Christmas with it on. He did shave if off (good thing, too, because he ended up in the hospital with the hiccups really bad for 13 hours on Christmas Eve. He left the hospital at 3 a.m. Christmas morning).

When Christopher moved to Arkansas, Len and I drove his cat Tiger to the new address. We were there to help Christopher get settled and his old pal was with him safe and sound. A year later, Len and I were there again to pack him up, and then drive back two cats, Tiger and his friend Arkansas. I have to say we did not have one bit of trouble with the cats.

When Christopher came home from Arkansas he went to work for the "Alliance for Disabled in Action, Inc." in Edison, NJ. It was a long ride from his condo each day.

In May of 2002 we had another addition to our family. Her name is Judy. She and Christopher got married in a beautiful ceremony May 3, 2002. It was very rewarding to see Christopher so happy and we welcome Judy with open arms.

MICHAEL,
MICHAEL, MOTORCYCLE

Michael was walking when he was hit by a drunk driver. He ended up in NICU at Temple University Hospital in Philadelphia for 49 days, then on to Magee Rehab in Philadelphia. Only six weeks at Magee because there was not much they could do for him physically. A lot of the training was for Leonard and I. Physically Michael had a big problem, but mentally he was very good. Magee taught him many valuable lessons, one was not to let anyone put a pill in your mouth unless you knew exactly what it if for, and you need to be able to talk a person through what to do for you in an emergency.

I have had a love/hate relationship with Magee. When it was time for Michael to get out of Temple we (Leonard and I), had to visit Rehabs around the Philadelphia area. Magee was really one of the best on the East Coast. Reporting back to Temple that this was where we wanted Michael to go, the social worker told me Magee was already on the phone to Temple saying that they did not want Michael there. The reason: "His Mother is unyielding."

"All the more reason that you should take Michael. His Mother will never desert him and you will never have any trouble about what to do with him."

Needless to say I learned very quickly what social workers do for a living. Magee did take Michael and any time he needed help in the next nine years of his life, Magee was there for Michael.

Would you believe this was December 1985 and in December 1986 arrangements were made for Christopher to go to Magee with his head injury? The doctor there said to me, "Mrs. Muka, I like you and your family very much, but please, I don't want all your business."

Michael went from Magee to a nursing home where there was another quad his age. During this time things were happening with Michael. There were news articles written about him, we learned how to do speeches, Michael and I went out to high schools, we were on TV a couple of times, etc., etc.

Michael asked that the boy who hit him not be sent to jail. His name was Bill Haydasz. Both Michael and Bill were 25 at the time. Bill got two months in jail, community service and a third thing. He had to go see Michael. That turned out to be the hardest thing for Bill to do.

For about a year he put it off. What finally pushed him to go to the nursing home to see Michael was a news article and picture on the front page of a newspaper that was delivered to Bill Haydasz's place. On the front page was a picture of Michael Muka, in his wheelchair, talking to high school students. Bill told us he just sat there looking at that picture, telling himself that Michael had gotten his life together and all he (Bill) was doing was sitting around. (By the way, when Michael was hit he was walking well off the side of a road, a road Michael walked every day home from work. A fireman had seen Michael moments before he was hit and said Michael was well off the road. Down the road firemen had to turn around their truck because there were wires across the road and they had to find another way to get to where they were going. So they passed Michael once again and saw him laying in a ditch. They made the choice to continue on to fight the fire that they were sent out to do on this rainy night but called in that there was someone hurt in the ditch, and got help for Michael).

Just about this time Michael finally got a power wheelchair. Even though Michael was a C4 quad incomplete C5, it was incomplete C5 because he had one bicep that could pull one arm up. His arm would drop and his hand would fall into a horse shoe, this way he could push and pull inside the horse shoe and work his power wheelchair. One of the happiest days I had during all this was when I arrived at the nursing home and Michael showed me his new chair he was tooling around in. Moments later he wanted to go talk to someone and said to me, "I'll be right back." Michael had legs.

One day, not long after, while looking out a window, Michael saw a young man walking up the long drive way to the nursing home. Michael could see sweat glistening on the young man's arms. Bill came into the lobby and asked at the desk for Michael Muka.

Bill told me later he expected Michael to come around the corner in his wheelchair screaming at him. Instead, Michael simply said, "Let's go for a walk." Outside they went, just quietly talking.

Our Michael said to Bill, "I have already forgiven you and now is the time to forgive yourself."

Bill had lost his driver license for two years, so to visit Michael he had to change to several kinds of transportation and did lot of walking.

After that, Bill came out with us to talk to the youth that would listen to us. We even did a night at Rider University. The Fireside Lounge was so packed people were sitting on the floor, standing room only. Security had to come and turn students away. Michael, Bill and I spoke and then asked if there were any questions.

The one I'll never forget was one that was asked of Bill, "Why in the world would you come here and do this?"

Bill pointed to me and said, "Because she asked me to. Could you say no to her?" Then he went on to say, you can always get the victim and maybe the parents, "But let me tell you, you won't always get the person who did it. I'm here to tell you not to put yourself in my position. I think about what I have done everyday."

It was October 1988 when Michael, Bill Haydasz and I put on the program "Drinking and Driving.. .It's a Fatal Attraction", at Rider College, now University. I have a bunch of news articles in No.8 scrapbook about the program.

Bill is now living with his parents. He has finished his college education at Temple University in Philadelphia. We kept in touch up until Michael died. My boss at the time called Bill, because she had met him earlier, to tell him that Michael had passed. I wrote him later and said unless he needed me I would not be writing anymore because I felt it was time for him to keep going on with a good life. BUT if he faltered, I would be there to kick him in the pants or words to that effect.

A note from my Mother about a TV program Michael and I did:

Think you missed your calling. You came over great on TV. Your voice was clear and in every way the program was well done. I'll take good care of the tape but want a copy made for keeps. Have a Happy Birthday. Pat yourself on the back for me. You're sure great - got a good back bone - - Thank God -
Like the head on your shoulders, too.

Love-Mother

It took me a while, but in the long run we got Michael close to us in his own condo, his own van, and his own aid to drive and take care of him 24 hours a day. The plate on Michael's van read "M. Muka." I had no trouble driving that van and did many times before I got his aid straightened out. The van was so large that Alexander thought the back of it was a room. (The van did have a bed in the back in case Michael needed it while out and away from home).

A friend from Rider, Kathy Burd, found a little, black kitten in a bush one day.

She gave it to our Michael. Michael named him "Shadow." A girl friend, Norma, took Shadow after Michael's death and Shadow went to live in Maryland.

Even though Michael could not lift a child, we would put the baby or young child on Michael's lap and put Michael's arm around the child and quick snap the picture. Michael seemed to enjoy that, part of the future. Pictures, pictures, pictures of everything. Pictures of Kimberly and Alexander looking out the front window of our house while standing on the couch. Watching Uncle Michael unloading from the big, red van. Same two kids ran and hid when Uncle Michael rolled into the living room. Michael loved it.

A few pages later in the scrapbooks there are pictures of when Leonard and I took

Mike Austin (Michael's aid) and Michael to Six Flags Great Adventure Theme Park and

Safari for Michael's last birthday with us. (Only we didn't know, of course, that it was going to be Michael's last birthday).

At every opportunity we had a gathering at Michael's. Wherever he was we would take over a large room and have a party. At the nursing home, at the English House apartments, at his condo we rented the club house. Michael and Christopher were never left out nor did they get away with not having parties at their places. We would bring the food, but they had to put up with the noise.

Michael died December 5, 1994 after his second stroke.

LAWRENCE

Lawrence and Malou were married in our home in Yardley, but after Feather came to this country Lawrence and Malou had a church wedding. Stephen came home from Chicago for the wedding. A picture of my sons was taken, the last picture of the five boys together. June 1983.

When Feather had her first birthday (7 years old) with us, we didn't have any little girls, so we had an adult birthday party for her. I had dozens of small, sterile, urine sample bottles from Michael. In Michael's condition they had to keep him catheterized so the hospital did not use these little bottles. Being MOM of course I took them home. I knew someday I would use them to save buttons in or something.

Well, here we are, going to have a birthday party for a 7-year-old girl, an adult party no less. I gave each person coming to the party one, two, sometimes three little plastic jars with lids. Each person had to fill up their jar/jars with gifts for a little girl. It was great. Some had little toys, some had dimes, some had candy, one had a watch, ribbons, beads, etc. It kept Feather busy and we had the party.

It turned out the Feather (Faye) had three parties that birthday: one with us, one with us and Malou's family and one with her classmates. Everyone was very happy Malou had her little girl with her safe and sound.

Kimberly was born November 19, 1986. Her big sister Faye went to Catholic Grammar School and I got to go to Grandmother's day at school. In the meantime, life went on. Around Easter Lawrence and Malou separated and in the end divorced. Lawrence has always been a father figure to Faye and a true father to Kimberly.

We had an Easter breakfast in 1988 at Englis House were Michael was now living in his apartment for the disabled with 24-hour care. They had a great room and would let us use it anytime as long as we made arrangements. Well, it was Easter, and all of Michael's family was there. I have a picture in the scrapbook No. 8 that shows Laura with Lawrence, Kimberly and Faye. It reminds me of what Evelyn, my sister-in-law, said to me. "OK Carolyn, I know I don't see you often enough, but don't tell me that girl over there with Lawrence is Malou?"

I just cracked up. It was the funniest thing I had heard in a long, long time (because Evelyn and I only got to see each other when it was a big family thing, I simple never thought to tell her about Lawrence and the divorce). I still think it is funny. If you could have seen Evelyn's face.

Lawrence and Laura got married on November 25, 1989 at the Hamilton Fitness Center, 133 Youngs Road, Mercerville, NJ, where they first met.

If you start to compare dates you will find that Michael just had a stroke shortly before this wedding. It was tough on the kids getting married, but we assured Laura that if you want to be in this family, this is just the way it works for us. Again, with a lot of help on Laura's side of the family, everything turned out beautifully. Dear Kimberly cried through the whole ceremony and Lawrence had to take her from me and hold her while getting married to Laura. Laura whispered something in Kimberly ear after it was over and Laura told me she said, "I'll get you for that or something to that effect." It was all in good nature, of course. Kimberly was only around two or so at that time and was still hanging onto her Dad's leg.

All the families were there from both sides. Leonard and I feel very blessed with our daughters-in-law, we feel that they are our daughters. Both sets of their parents are of course just great. Everyone over the years have proven to be really good people.

Ted and Dot Rettman, (Laura's parents) have always treated Kimberly like their own grandchild. Over the years, Laura, and her two sisters, Robin and Lisa have added to Rettman grandchildren by another five girls and two boy grandbabies

We, (Leonard and I) were living at 470 Miller Avenue, Trenton, NJ by now, during this time. We had an apartment made upstairs. Guess who was living in our apartment for their first two years? Our Laura and Lawrence, of course.

At St. John The Evangelist Church, on March 29, 1990, "Faye Maria Francisco" received the Sacrament of Confirmation in the Catholic Church. Christmas 1990 was upstairs in Laura and Lawrence's apartment in the AM and dinner downstairs early afternoon in our country kitchen.

June 1991 Lisa and Bill got married --Laura's sister.

We had given Lawrence a basketball set for one of his birthday and he didn't put it up so Leonard and I asked for it back and it went up at 470 Miller Avenue. We had some heated good times out there.

We had a pizza party in Laura and Lawrence's first home in Morrisville, PA, the first night they were there, Winding Way. That Christmas there was a Santa who visited Laura and Lawrence's new home and would you believe there just happened to be a bunch of kids there? With a grill outside and lots of love going around there were three beautiful children born to Laura and Lawrence as the years rolled by in that home - Darian, Eliot and Nathaniel. Every Wednesday night and every other weekend Kimberly gets to be with her extended family and with Faye it is really complete. Faye graduated in May 2003 from Temple University in Philadelphia, PA.

DARIAN KENNEDY MUKA was born March 18, 1993. Faye and Kimberly made all sorts of beautiful signs to welcome home Darian and Laura. Alexander, (Magda and James' son, born May 1990), liked the new baby also. Five months later when Nicholette was born, Alexander had his own little baby sister. Aunt

Betty was particularly taken with Darian because Darian had the same blood condition that Aunt Betty, Leonard, and Lawrence had. Aunt Betty left a letter for Darian, taped to the back of a shadow box that Laura's wedding bouquet had been framed in for Darian to keep. Aunt Betty knew that it would not be long before she would die and would not get to know Darian. In December 1993 Betty passed from the cancer she had. Darian' s first visit to Grandmom and Grandpop Muka's house was on Easter morning 1993. (I'm sure she remembers).

Laura and Lawrence had an in-ground pool in their backyard. On the day of Darian's baptism there was a big party and lots of people in the pool - even Darian and she was only 4 months old.

Our little Darian and Nicholette got along right off. They are like sisters, more like twins. On Darian's 1st birthday, Aunt Magda and Grandmom Muka took Darian to the doctor and had her ears pierced and bought her little gold earrings.

As you open up scrapbook No.14 there is a note from Lawrence, which was left on our kitchen table for Len and I to find: 9/94. It said:

> *Mom/Dad,*
> *Used your phone and ate your food.*
> *Thanks,*
> *Lawrence.*

(P.S. Thanks for helping my brother Michael)

MICHAEL DIED DECEMBER 5, 1994

Our little Darian took her first ride in a limo when her Uncle Michael was buried. I know because I took pictures of her. Laura really wanted to take pictures of Darian's first limo ride, but Lawrence said, "NO. You'll upset my Mother." And, of course, while this was going on, I walked out of the house with camera in hand

86

to take pictures of our Darian and her first time in a limo. That's when Laura said, "See, I knew it would be all right. I knew it would be all right."

I have kept some special notes from the grandchildren, especially one from Darian, which read: "To Gen Pop and Gen Mom. I love you." By the way, did I mention that our Darian Kennedy Muka just happens to have very fair skin, green eyes and red hair? A "Kennedy."

Our little Darian ended up with the same blood condition that Leonard and Lawrence had. In all three it meant that their spleens had to be removed. Darian was only 5 years old. She was sick on and off her whole young life when she had her gall bladder and spleen removed at the same time. She really went through a bad time of it. I give Laura and Lawrence a lot of credit that they had more children. Eliot did not have a trace of this, but his yet to be born little brother has it. Nathaniel is now 2 ½ years old (at this writing) but is a healthy boy, not sick like Darian was. In the end, I am sure he will have to have his spleen removed, but not until it starts to bother him.

We (Leonard and I) had six children and only Lawrence had this blood condition. Lawrence he had four children: Kimberly, Darian, Eliot and Nathaniel. It is Darian and Nathaniel who have it now.

I have written in my scrapbook No.19 on the inside front cover:
Darian went to Children's Hospital on this day, to correct her first operation. With the wise decision of her parents and the grace of God we still have Darian with us. Grandmom Muka babysat Kimberly and Eliot. It was a long day. A tired Lawrence picked up the children very late, while Laura stayed in Philadelphia with our Darian.

In 1995, Laura and Lawrence had Thanksgiving at their home. In order to have both families, there was a table in the sun room, dinning room, living room and kitchen. Needless to say, we have since split up a bit. If it is coffee and cake that's great but if it is opening gifts at Christmas, big dinners, etc., we have taken turns around different homes on different days. The summer is one time it works for everyone because half of the people are outside.

Christmas 1995 Faye got her white afghan from her Grandmom Muka. It is my goal to make one for each child. Kimberly has her purple one and now for his 12th birthday Alexander has his red one (red because Alexander is color blind and red, bright red, is one color he can see). I still have Darian, Nicholette, Eliot and Nathaniel to do. That Christmas Darian got a big red wagon for Christmas.

In December 1995 we had a new grandson, Eliot, who was born to Laura and Lawrence. A beautiful boy. Now we had an oldest grandson Alexander and a youngest grandson Eliot. We gave Eliot golf clubs as a gift when he was born - real golf clubs, but for a young child. I wonder if he ever used them?

At this point our Faye graduated from High School, and of course there were those prom pictures, etc. She has always been a beautiful child and now a beautiful young woman.

I made Eliot's Christening outfit from his Nanna's wedding gown. Eliot's Godparents were: Bill Martino, Laura's brother-in-law and Christopher Muka, Lawrence's brother. I think Eliot is lucky to have two guys for God parents.

June 1996 Kimberly received her First Holy Communion. We gave her a beautiful birthstone ring. Kimberly also took dance lessons and was in "Best Sellers" in June of 1997. There are lots of little parties for all the little kids, they make for good pictures.

One day Lawrence brought in a camera crew from Rider College (Barry James) to our 470 Miller home and they shot a commercial, EYE Inc., President – Lawrence L. Muka.

The Mercer County Chamber of Commerce had a very nice article about "Motivated Collegian Custodians" with a picture of Lawrence.

**MOTIVATED COLLEGIAN CUSTODIANS,
P0 BOX 7422, W. TRENTON, NJ**
Provide regular janitorial services by college students
who are strong in motivation, intelligence, discipline and
physical endurance. The company picks up and returns
the students to campus and supervises their work on
the premises. Service is provided seven days a week, 24-
hours-a-day, contracted on any schedule desired. Special
jobs can be sub-contracted. In business only a year, the
company now has about 24 clients, including government
complexes and education buildings. All workers are in-
sured and bonded when necessary. Future plans include
service in lawn care, parking lot supervision, snow and
trash removal, painting, laundry and security work. Clients are located mainly in Princeton, Mercer and Bucks
counties. Lawrence L. Muka is president.

**Need a job? Call 911 WORK
(News article in the Times, Saturday July 20, 1998)**

HAMILTON -
In the spare room of their parents' Hamilton home, Lawrence
Muka and brothers James and Christopher operate a cross between
an employment agency and an answering service. (Guess who answered the phone when THEY were not around?)
Let us not forget, CAREER FAX, and the JCL GROUP, INC.,or
maybe we do want to forget about it?
A while after, we moved to a Senior Citizen Apartment Building and ended up on the eighth floor. How about that for a
change? That is where the babysitting came to an end. (One day
when I was still babysitting - and on the eighth floor - and Laura
was coming across the parking lot to pick up Darian and Eliot, I
had the kids yell down to their Mom, "Mom come get us out of
here," over and over, real loud. The kids had a ball and I thought
it was funny.

89

By this time, Lawrence was working for the State of New Jersey as a CNE (Certified Network Engineer). He is still there doing a great job. Of course, when he gets to our home I have a list of things for him to fix on my computer.

In October 1998 there was a trip to Disney in Florida. Lawrence asked if everyone (Lawrence, Laura, kids and Laura's whole family) could come down to the shore house and sleep over one night and take off early the next morning because Long Beach Island was so close to the Atlantic City Airport. (You can see why Len and I didn't mind the eighth floor of a Senior Citizen Apartment Building with a shore house to go to every weekend). So 17 people came and slept over, spent their vacation at Disney and came back to the shore house after the trip. Most of them stayed over night again and went home the next day We got a lovely note from Lawrence on our return to our shore house:

Mom and Dad,

Sorry about the mess. We are so late.
The table and benches look great.

Lawrence

Guess what we got on July 27, 2000? A little boy named Nathaniel Parrish Muka. A little boy who was born with brown eyes that are still dark brown and beautiful. Now, our Eliot is the big brother and Nathaniel is the little brother. Nathaniel is a most pleasant child. Nathaniel wore a knitted Christening outfit that I made for his Christening. He was so cute. Magda and Lisa were God parents for Nathaniel.

A first birthday party for Nathaniel was at Laura and Lawrence's backyard pooi and there was room for all. Christmas that year we were greeted at their front door by a rug which read: 'THE MUKAS. Where the women are strong, the men are good looking, and all the children are above average." Pretty good. I liked it. One of Laura's sisters had it made for them.

> (Lawrence may not want to hear this,
> but I think he is the son most like me).

JAMES

When Stephen called and told us about his Hodgkin's Disease in 1978, it was a Sunday. The next day, James was leaving for Bishop Egan High School. He paused for a moment and asked me, "Mom, you are not going to let this get you down are you? If Stephen gets better it's OK, and if Stephen doesn't get better he goes to heaven. What more do you want from us guys?" (From the youngest son. Thanks, James.)

EGAN, WOOD CAGERS GAIN PCL STAR SLOTS 2/24/82

PHILADELPHIA -- Two members each of the Bishop Egan and Archbishop Wood High Schools boys basketball teams were chosen by the coaches last night to spots on the Philadelphia Catholic League's All-Star Team. Garnering third-team honors were Egan's Bob Molle, a senior, and Archbishop Wood's John Iannarelli, also a senior. Honorable mention went to Egan's Jim Muka and Wood's Bill Boyk.

SPOTLIGHT -This issue's Spotlight focuses on James L. Muka. James is a Certified Public Accountant who is in his second year with Jump, Bowe and Company. He joined our Firm in January 1987, after two years with a CPA firn in Trenton. We are fortunate to be able to utilize the combined computer and accounting skills of James to broaden our services to our clients. James spends virtually all of his time installing computer accounting packages and "troubleshooting" computer application problems.

James is a 1986 graduate of Rider College, with a Bachelor of Science degree in accounting. He resides in Plainsboro with his wife, Magda. James' personal interests include golfing and basketball.

In our travels through time, let's not forget:
"QUALITY PAINTING AT REASONABLE RATES"
Call the "UP FOR GRADS" PAINTING SERVICE.
Christopher 215-736-9193, James 215-493-1653
(Well, it did keep them out of trouble for one summer at least.)

The Dean's list at Rider College, 1984, included Christopher Muka and James Muka.

Magda and James had gotten married while working down the shore the summer after James' junior year at college. Later, they had a big wedding for all the families to attend.

Magda and James had a beautiful church wedding. It was one of Michael's first outings. Some how, with the help of an aid, rented van, etc. we got Michael to Trenton. It was great. From then on, there was no holding this family down. No matter what we looked like to other people, WE WERE OUT THERE.

Len and I had sold our home in Yardley and were living in a second floor, two-bedroom apartment in Ewing, Trenton, N.J. when Magda and James first got married. Shortly after that Len had to go away on a sales job for a couple of days. I asked James and Magda, (who were living on Rider College Campus at the time), to come stay with me in the apartment for a few nights while Leonard was away. THEY STAYED TWO YEARS.

Magda and James are Kimberly's Godparents. Magda and James both got through Rider - James graduating in February, 1987. James passed his CPA test the first chance he was allowed to take it. We gave him a surprise party and it was truly a surprise. James got a job with Robert Allen as a Certified Public Accountant in Mercerville, NJ. Later, James went to work for Jump, Bowe and Company in Toms River.

Now, one of the good times. Magda and James were going to finally have a baby. It turned out to be Alexander James Muka in May 1990. There was a baby shower, etc., and a Baptism in St. Rose of Lima Church, Freehold, NJ. Jackie and Ranardo were the Godparents, (Magda's brother and wife). Everyone was there including my two sisters (Marlene and Patty). We had our pictures taken up at the altar because each one of us ladies had been baptised in St. Rose of Lima Church, Freehold, NJ.

I got to care for baby Alexander during the day, the first year of his life. (Care to see the pictures? I have a few.) One day after Alexander was walking, I could not find the remote to the TV anywhere. Finally, I got down on my knees to see where the wee one might have put it. As I looked around I saw the kitchen oven. Naa it couldn't be in there. SURE ENOUGH IT WAS.

Summer of 1993 Grandpa, Christopher and Alexander went out and played golf. I just went around and tried to hold every one up. That was tough because they all kept wanting to sit down (one 70+ man, one handicapped male adult and one tired little boy)...

A couple of times, when he was very young, Alexander made a Charlotte's web in the kitchen (of our 470 Miller home) with the help of the kitchen chairs. Later, when he was a little older, it was the deck outside with the porch furniture. I have fond memories of when Alexander's father made a large one down in our family room in our Yardley house, when he was young.

When Michael was forced to go to Magee on occasion other than his checks ups, and I was babysitting Alexander, Alexander would just come along with Len and I.

In fact, when I signed the papers for Michael's condo, Alexander was with me. Gordon Graves drove and Dick Daly babysat while I took care of Michael's business.

By now, James and Magda had a nice townhouse in Freehold, NJ. Alexander's first birthday party was a barbecue at the Freehold home.

No surprise that on Halloween 1992 Alexander was a doctor, Magda a cowgirl and James a bum. On Alexander's 3rd birthday, we

95

grandparents gave Alexander a pair of red cowboy boots (just like mine) and Christopher gave Alexander a cowboy hat. I was invited to his nursery school party and went. After that, I didn't attend too many kid's parties. I like sticking to the home stuff. Besides, I learned a lesson at that party. You have to let the grandchildren go. Even at that age their friends were very important to them. After all, you always have grandparents. Life goes on. Really, I had to grow up a little at that point. I surprised myself about how jealous I was that he hardly noticed me. "Poor Me."

Usually Alexander helped me put up the nativity set at Christmas time.That lasted for a few years, but he has since outgrown that, too. (As of this writing, Alexander will be a teenager in May 2003). Do you think I should give him a break?

As I am going thru the scrapbooks, I see that I have pictures of Alexander that I could black-mail him with. Maybe I'll just keep them for when he starts to bring the girls around.

Also, I have a picture of one of those famous breakfasts, a pie pan with two eggs, liver worst and hard roll. "Just like the bakery," as James would say.

There was a time we could not use our dining room table (that was in the country kitchen, 470 Miller Avenue) because one of our kids started a family business called the RNDex cards. I won't mention which KID it was. I have a great shot of Magda doing RNDex cards. but not alone. Lawrence was helping, but not alone. Right beside him is our Laura working and it looks like she is just about due to have her baby – Darian. A family that works together, stays together or something like that. The RNDex cards are just a memory now.

On one of James' grownup birthdays we gave him a "sea horse" a live one in an aquarium with sea water in it. James had to take it home to his Freehold, NJ house. James always wanted one, so now he had it. I got the sea horse back the next Christmas, only it was hard and stuck to a safety pin for me to wear. He got it back in a shadow box to hang on the wall. Come to think of it I haven't seen that thing since.

Magda worked for Squibb and sometimes she would let me make some fun things for her to give away - real expensive things like recycling baby food jars with red candy in them with a painted red lid and a little American flag for July. Or there were the mini teddy bears made with cheap material and I would sew and stuff them and Magda would paint a face on them. It kept me busy and out of trouble. Squibb, of course, does not do anything like that anymore

MUKA DEVELOPMENT GROUP, LLC ANNOUNCES:

The addition of Magda C. Muka to Muka Development Group. For the past 13 years, Magda has held various positions within Bristol-Myers Squibb including sales, marketing and sales force automation. Magda trail blazed the roll-out of laptop computers to 400+ sales representatives. She worked with vendors on software development, and managed training and support. Magda's addition to Muka Development will surly enhance the quality of services that we provide you.

Sincerely,
James L. Muka

Alexander started in the Pop Warner, Howell Lions Football No. 20 and each year just got better and better. There aren't words enough to say the enjoyment he has given to his Grandpop. His Grandpop liked to yell and at Alexander's games Len could yell his head off, and I swear it was good for his heart. With all the health problems Leonard had, when it came to Alexander's football you would never have known it. I think it is one of the things that kept Len alive.

Muka Development Group has done very well, and now there is a great big house in Farmingdale, NJ with an in-ground pool. Magda and James have had a big pool party each year for any member of the families who choose to come (and all of the kids of course). They turned out to be really good times. If you put the pictures from one year to the next together, you could not tell the year except for which kid had front teeth and which kid didn't. Every year there are improvements: hot tub, iron fence around pool, water falls, trees, etc. Their home and yard has really shaped up nicely.

A few months before Aunt Betty died, God gave our family a little baby girl, Nicholette. Nicholette was born August 31, 1993. One day, towards the end, Nicholette came to visit Aunt Betty. We put baby Nicci close to Aunt Betty in bed, and you should have seen the smile on Betty's face. During that last illness, the children could always get Aunt Betty to smile. We did not shield the children from anything, this was life. Betty wanted to die at home with us and that is the way it happened with the help of SMARTTAN HOSPICE.

The winter of 1993-94 brought a lot of snow and low temperatures. It also brought the Christening of "Nicholette Angelica Muka." Laura and Lawrence were Nicci's God parents. Nicholette turned into a beautiful baby. Alexander was pretty good with his little sister. In fact, he is still pretty good with her.

Nicholette's 1st birthday party was at their home in Freehold. Nicholette just loved it. Automatic smile every time the camera came around. There were all sorts of little grandchildren running around: Kimberly, Alexander, Darian and Nicholette.

At Nicholette's 2nd birthday, Magda and her Mom Francis had a large roasted pig. And yes, with an apple in its mouth for Nicholette's guests. Again, Nicholette just loved everything, especially the cake. This was still in the Freehold Townhouse.

Life goes on. A few years later came the big house in Farmingdale, a few more cousins: ELIOT AND NATHANIEL. How blessed Len and I are.

James, the youngest of the Muka boys,who was never the baby of the family.

RIDER

Working at Rider College in Lawrenceville, NJ proved to be very good for me. I enjoyed my time there and everyone was so supportive of me when I needed it most. Family, friends, following sports, trips, and most of all God, helped us through those good and bad days. Some great bosses didn't hurt either: Wilson Myres, John B. Carpenter and Cassie Iacovelli. I once told Mr. Carpenter that I was operating with half a deck but everything turned out well at work, because John B. Carpenter had the other half a deck.

(Len broke an ankle at a ladies basketball game in Lehigh, PA. I forget who won. All I know is Len was on crutches for the next six weeks. (We are true fans as we have been back since for Rider vs. Lehigh.)

Date:October 6, 1988
To: Campus Community
From: Frank N. Elliott, President
Re: Alcohol Awareness Week

Rider College along with many colleges throughout the country will be celebrating National Alcohol Awareness Week during the week of October 17-24, 1988. Many educational programs will be sponsored here at Rider College to heighten the awareness of the students, faculty, and administration to their drinking habits. This year's theme is "Drinking and Driving... A Fatal Attraction."

One particularly impactive program during this week is entitled "Drinking and Driving - — The Consequences — A True Story" scheduled for Tuesday, October 18, 1988 at 8 p.m.in the Student Center Theater. This program is a human drama which deals with Carolyn Muka, a college employee, and her family's own personal tragedy as a result of drinking and driving.

On July 22, 1985, Michael Muka (Carolyn's son) was walking down a road. Bill Haydasz, a reporter who consumed too much alcohol and was driving, came down the same road and hit Michael. Michael will be a quadriplegic for life. Bill's life was also changed drastically and will never be the same again.

On October 18, 1988, Michael Muka, Bill Haydasz, and Carolyn Muka will share their story. This is the first time these three people will do this kind of a program and yet they feel they have a powerful message to share with the Rider College community. I encourage you to attend this important program.

There have probably been as many as fifteen alcohol-related drinking deaths of Rider students during the past nineteen years. We cannot afford to suffer any more losses. Take the time during Alcohol Awareness Week to reconsider your drinking habits and please encourage the students you associate with to do the same.

F.N.Elliott

CAMPUS LIVING October 14, 1988 –

DRIVER AND VICTIM TELL STORY LECTURE TO REVEAL A TRAGEDY

By Pat Lewis

While many people have seen a lecture about the dangers of drunk driving, few people have seen a lecture about a paralyzed man in a wheelchair facing the man who put him there, according to Cassie Iacovelli, director of Student Activities. Michael Muka, 28, was struck by a car driven by Bill Haydasz, also 28. They have created a classic opportunity to teach the audience about the dangers of drinking and driving, Iacovelli said.

The lecture on Tuesday in the Student Center Theater will be an early climax of the Alcohol Awareness Week, aptly titled, "Drinking and Driving: A Fatal Attraction."

Michael was struck by the car, leaving him almost totally paralyzed from the neck down during the summer of 1985.

Michael's mother, Carolyn Muka, works in the Student Center and is in charge of booking reservations. Iacovelli displayed a passionate drive to make students take the opportunity to witness the human drama. "We could not do the program if we did not have access to three people to draw on here," Iacovelli said. She added, "Carolyn decided not to sensationalize the story. She could have sued Bill Haydasz for a lot of money to help alleviate the doctor bills, but she did not."

Muka described the ordeal her son endured. Three years ago Michael Muka was struck by Haydasz's car while walking home from work. He merely had his six foot-eight inch frame to protect him from that car that summer night. Muka continued, "As the chief of police drove by he saw Michael lying in the grass away from the road. After the chief had Michael taken to a hospital, he found Bill Haydasz at a separate accident miles away. If no one had found Michael, he would have died there."

101

Muka said that at the time, the police determined Haydasz had a blood alcohol content of .24, (the legal limit is .10) Haydasz did not even know he had hit someone with his car, Muka added. "At the time of the accident," she said, "Haydasz was a confirmed alcoholic. It was not until he saw a picture of Michael strapped to a wheelchair that he decided to turn over a new leaf."

Muka said she did not know where her son got the strength to forgive Haydasz before the trial. "Neither Michael or I thought about our feelings toward Bill Haydasz.." Muka said that Haydasz was sentenced to two months in Bucks County Prison in Doylestown, Pennsylvania for leaving the scene of an accident and driving drunk. She said he also was sentenced to do 200 hours of institutional type work.

Muka said her son asked for a lenient sentence for Haydasz. "At the time of the trial," she said, "Michael asked to meet Haydasz later on. About a year and a half later, Michael saw Haydasz approaching him one day while Michael's aid was pushing him in his wheelchair outdoors.

Muka said that her son asked Haydsaz to go for a walk with him. "Mike comforted Bill. Mike said, 'Forgive yourself because I have forgiven you.'"

Muka said her son is one of five percent of all quadriplegics who have some feeling in their bodies, specifically Michael, his right bicep. He has learned to bring food to his mouth and write his signature. Michael has only 70 percent of his lung capacity, and people find it hard to understand him."

Michael was struck by the car, leaving him almost totally paralyzed from the neck down during the summer of 1985, a C4 incomplete C5 right arm.

Carolyn Muka said, "The audience will be drawn into the drama, but they don't have to deal with the story after they leave the lecture. When the night is over, Bill and Michael will still deal with it."

RIDER COLLEGE: Tom Hofmann

Rider plans alcohol awareness programs

LAWRENCE - Rider College will sponsor its fifth annual Alcohol Awareness Week in conjunction with National Collegiate Alcohol Awareness Week beginning Monday.

The intent of Alcohol Awareness Week is to increase overall knowledge regarding alcohol consumption and the potential dangers associated with it.

Cassie Iacovelli, Rider's Director of Student Activities, began the program because she felt that "(drinking) was an area that needed more attention." Until last year, students were the sole focus of the event. However, the scope of the program has been increased.

"THE ORIGINAL" purpose of Alcohol Awareness Week was to challenge students to become more responsible drinkers, but we broadened it last year to include faculty and administration as well," said Iacovelli.

This year's affair will focus specifically on the perils of drinking and driving. The theme for the event is "Drinking and Driving: A Fatal Attraction." The most dramatic activity of the week occurs on Tuesday, when some courageous people will participate in a lecture in the Student Center Theater at 8 p.m. Rider College employee Carolyn Muka will be present along with her son Michael. Michael was the victim of a drunken, hit-and-run driver several years ago and has been a quadriplegic ever since. Bill Haydasz, the driver of the vehicle that struck Michael Muka, will also take part in the activity.

Rider students and employees will have the opportunity to see and hear both victim and driver of the alcohol-related accident. Iacovelli hopes that the appearance of these people and the discussion of how their lives have been affected will serve to illustrate the dangers of mixing drinking and driving more clearly than any literature could.

HOWEVER, there will also be other methods used in the attempt to increase awareness. Resident assistants etc. etc. etc...

OCTOBER 18, 1988
"FATAL ATTRACTION PROGRAM" took place.

Written by hand was a letter from Rider's president.
October 18, 1988
From the President of Rider College,
Frank Elliott

Dear Carolyn:

As I told Mike, I watched and admired three very strong and courageous people this evening!

Mike was, and is, a handsome giant of a man. He's confined in stature but I think he must also have grown in stature. I don't know that I would forgive as you and he have forgiven. Yet, the fact that you had, so obviously really had, made the evening so powerful.

I feel absolutely confident that as a result of tonight's session at least one person in that audience wll not, someday, sit in one of those three seats.

Thank you!
F.E.

October 19, 1988
Mrs. Carolyn Muka
Student Activities Office
Rider College

Dear Carolyn:

You are truly a remarkable person! Last night's program which you conceived, produced, directed and co-starred in was one of the most powerful programs I have ever seen at Rider or anywhere else.

104

I know that it touched the jam-packed audience very deeply. If it touched us as deeply as I believe it did, you will never know how many similar tragedies it may have prevented. If it failed to reach any of us who were there, I hope that you will never know that either. In any case, I hope that you are very proud of the courage and commitment demonstrated by Carolyn, Michael and Bill in your effort to prevent other young people and their families from suffering a similar tragedy.

With sincere gratitude and appreciation,
I am, Sincerely yours,
James M. McRoberts – Vice President for Student Affairs

MEMORANDUM – October 21, 1988
To: Carolyn Muka
By: Cassie D. Iacovelli
Re: Program for Alcohol Awareness Week

I want to thank you for allowing me to present your family's tragedy to impact Rider College during Alcohol Awareness Week. There is no disputing, the program would not have occurred without you. Your willingness to contact Bill and Michael, your support in orchestrating the evening's format and your unbelievable ability to show strength enough to participate, allowed me to present the most dramatic, educational and soul-searching program in my life as a college professional.

I know your story touched lives. So many people have approached me to comment on the intensity of Tuesday evening's program. I was delighted with the attendance from the Rider College community, especially the large turn-out from the students. I can only hope you felt a sense of accomplishment about the evening's program. I was so proud to say I worked with you in Student Activities.

I know this has been a tough couple of months for you in Student Activities and that's why I appreciate even more your willingness to support a Student Activities program.

You are one in a million. Rider College is very lucky to have you as an employee andStudent Activities is even luckier to have you on our team.

I know in my heart, the program on Tuesday will save lives. Thanks for caring enough to send your family's message.

October 21, 1988
Bill Haydasz
8114 Elberon Avenue
Philadelphia, PA 19111

Dear Bill,

I know I have said this to you verbally, but I want to again thank you for your powerful role on Tuesday, October 18, 1988 at Rider College in our Alcohol Awareness Week program.

I have had so many people approach me to commend the efforts of Tuesday's program. The impact of the program and the most valuable message from the program could not have occurred without you. I know you find it ironic to be labeled "courageous" but in this instance, you were. To face Michael and Carolyn publicly and then Rider College took tremendous courage.

I know what you said will leave an impression with the Rider College community. I also know in my heart, the program's message will save lives. Never underestimate the truly valuable contribution you have made on so many people's lives. I will never be able to thank you enough.

In closing, the Tuesday evening program was the most impactful and dramatic event I have sponsored in my twelve years as a college administrator. Without you, the program would never have been possible. The message needs to be heard, but without a messenger, there is no message and people will continue to die because of drinking and driving. Thank you for taking time out of your schedule - to care.

Sincerely,
Cassie D. Iacovelli
Director, Student Activities

October25, 1988
Michael Muka
Apartment #204
2610 Belmont Avenue
Philadelphia, PA 19131

Dear Michael,

I want to express my sincere appreciation for your role in the Alcohol Awareness program on Tuesday, October 18, 1988 here at Rider College. I recognize a trip to the college required some extensive planning and it is for this reason that I appreciate even more your involvement in our program.

I have had so many people seek me out to commend this program. As much as I enjoy the feedback, I realize the program could not have occurred without you. The impact of your side of the story provided the reality of the effects of drinking and driving. You shared your story with such honesty and candidness and it will leave a lasting impression on the people who attended the program.

As I've said to your mom and Bill, I know in my heart your lecture will save lives. Your message needs to be heard but it needs courageous people like you who are willing to spread the word. This was the most dramatic and dynamic program I have ever sponsored in my twelve years as a college administrator. I can't thank you enough for taking time out of your schedule - to care. As the coordinator of Alcohol Awareness with a vision to influence people about their drinking habits - the lecture on Tuesday far surpassed my expectations. Again, thank you for your very effective lecture.

Sincerely, Cassie D. Iacovelli, Director, Student Activities

ARTICLE IN THE TIMES, TRENTON, NJ, October 20, 1988 - By Arnold Ropeik

If you were on the Rider College campus Tuesday night your heart rode a roller coaster.

It began for me in the small theater in the new School of Business building. There, a group of leaders and supporters of the Holocaust/Genocide Resource Center gathered to honor a man who believes in human equality and put his actions where his soul was.

It concluded across the quadrangle in the Student Center where two young men and one of this world's outstanding women faced a packed house to throw the harsh light of reality on the problem of drunken driving.

IN THE FIRST of the two sessions, Leonard DiDonato, a Lawrenceville resident, was honored by the Resource Center with its first Humanitarian Award. This Spring, Adath Israel Congregation erected a sign along Route 206 which announced the congregation's plans to build a sanctuary there. The cold winds of Hitler's time were felt when vandals painted swastikas and anti-Semitic epithets on the sign.

DiDonato, saddened to realize that hundreds of cars and maybe thousands of people had passed the defaced sign and had done nothing, brought paint removers and thinners to the sign and, in a slashing rain and sleet storm, scrubbed it clean.

All of the churches in the township were part of last night's salute and a number of tributes were voiced, including a profound thank you from Adath's Rabbi Daniel Grossman.

But Len DiDonato had the last word, challenging the room to work for a world where man gets along with man and God is a universal color.

That event over, I hurried to the Fireside Lounge of the Student Center and had to squeeze and twist to get into the room. When I finally made it, I looked at the faces in the crowd.

It was a palette of emotion, kids staring intently at the speakers, some with their knuckles in their mouths, others on the edge of their seats, some trying to appear casual, all held firmly in the vise of human tension. The room was very quiet.

On the makeshift podium were three people, Michael Muka, his mother Carolyn, and his friend, Bill Haydasz.

Three years ago Bill Haydasz, driving while drunk, struck Michael Muka down and left him paralyzed for life. You would understand if there was great sadness, bitterness, anger in the Muka family.

You would understand if Bill never wanted to go near Michael again and vice versa.

But that is not the way this drama is being played out. Friends before the accident, they remain so.

LOOKING at the faces of the young collegians, you could read astonishment, pride, love, comprehension, puzzlement and fear as they listened to how the Muka family forgave Bill, urged leniency for him by the court and played a part in reuniting the two so both could get on with the sometimes painful business of living.

One young man rose to concede that he would have had trouble handling it the way Muka and Haydasz did. Many gentle voices thanked the three.

I later told Bill that I thought he had courage to sit beside Michael and face an audience with the truth. He thought the word courage was not the right word. He thought it was just "guts," and that the word courage should be used for others.

Surely, Michael's uninjured sense of humor continued to wash over the room, the often nervous laughter softening the truth.

And though it all sat Carolyn Muka, the glue that binds them all together, outwardly calm, always reassuring, ever seeing the positive side. The crowd expressed its love for her vocally. I was proud of the kids who let their tears fall.

Two unforgettable events, proving that human beings do care deeply for each other after all.

Arnold Ropeik is senior editor of the Times, Trenton, NJ.

RIDER CAMPUS LIVING
October 21, 1988
By Cathy Anderson

When he started walking home that summer night in *1985,* Michael Muka could not have guessed that his friend, with whom he had been drinking minutes before, would be the driver of a car that would strike him, leaving him paralyzed for life.

Michael's friend, Bill Haydasz, had offered to drive him home, but he refused, opting to walk, because "I knew he was too drunk."

The two, both 25 years old at the time, lived within a mile of the Bucks County, Pa. bar where they came to drink that night, and frequently saw each other after work.

Bill explained, "I walked out of the bar. I didn't stumble. I started the car up. That's how I knew I wasn't too drunk."

Muka and Haydasz remain friends to this day, and they, along with Michael's mother, Carolyn Muka, addressed a crowd of about 300 students, faculty and administration at Rider College Tuesday evening as part of the college's Alcohol Awareness Week.

Muka forgave Haydasz for that tragic night. In fact, he asked the judge to give him a lenient sentence, despite the fact that Haydasz's blood alcohol level was at .285, well above the legal limit of. .10 at the time of the accident.

Carolyn Muka said, "We forgave him right away. Our family didn't have time to give Bill any of our energy, pro or con."

Haydasz served a two-month term in Bucks County Prison in Doylestown Borough, Pa.

After the accident, Muka took it upon himself to try to reach Haydasz. "I wanted to put his mind at ease," he explained.

Muka said he woke up saying, "1 forgive the person who did this to me.. .only because I could have been driving. If I lived farther away, I probably would have been driving, and I might have hit someone."

Haydasz said, however, that he did not want to see Muka. "I just blew it off. I didn't want to deal with it. I kept putting it out of my mind."

That is, until he opened the morning paper more than a year later and saw a picture of Muka strapped to his wheelchair. "I realized it wasn't something I could hide from. He was handling it better than I was," Haydasz said.

A quadriplegic, Muka was in the hospital for six months and then in a nursing home for a year, following the accident. He has been living in his own apartment for more than a year now, but he needs around-the-clock care.

Explaining why the family decided to put Michael into a nursing home instead of bring him to the family home when he left the hospital, Carolyn Muka said, "In the end, you've got to do it yourself Michael had to stand alone, even if it was in his wheelchair."

She explained that nothing her son does is spontaneous. "Everything is planned. Everything is a big event."

According to Michael Muka, the accident was a sobering experience, and has changed both his and Haydasz's lives for the better. He explained, "I've become a better person for it. Before, I was always number one. Now, having someone around to take care of me is always number one."

111

He added that they came to Rider last night to "let people know it could be the guy sitting next to you, anywhere. If they're drinking, they can be the one who will hit you." Haydasz said, from his point of view, "it could be you who's driving."

ONE FOR THE ROAD
March 24, 1988
Temple University News
By William J. Haydasz

I am an alcoholic.

I first got drunk when I was *15,* on a quart of warm beer.

At 17, I was drinking regularly, sharing pints of Bacardi 151 each Saturday night with two friends. I watched one of them vomit blood on his kitchen floor after a day of heavy drinking.

I was an alcoholic. You wouldn't have known to look at me.

In high school, I played basketball and got straight As. I was junior class president and a National Merit Scholar. My SAT score was 1400. I planned to go to medical school.

In college, I learned to drink cheaply. Almost every night there was a keg somewhere. My friends were all partiers. We kept each other informed. "Where are you drinking tonight?"

I managed to get by without studying. Drinking was more important than school.

I changed majors three times, giving my parents a different excuse each time. I dropped out as a senior, re-enrolled, and dropped out again.

My family couldn't understand what had happened, and I couldn't tell them. I moved four hours from home so I wouldn't have to explain myself to people who care about me.

I got a restaurant job and drank to "wind down" after work. On my nights off I drank to "have a good time."

A friend and I became regulars at an "old-man's bar." He would point to the all-day drinkers with their shots and beers and say, "That's us in 20 years." We would laugh. Those were alcoholics.

I wasn't, I thought. I never missed work or went to work drunk. I didn't drink during the day, and I didn't need to drink every night. And I usually drank just beer.

My friends drove me home one night when they thought I was too drunk to drive. I walked back to my car, and drove it into a tree.

My parents gave me their old car. I told myself I'd be more careful, and not get so drunk. I resolved to cut down.

I started going to a bar closer to home - a shorter drive - and began to drink more.

One night I left the bar and got in my car. I realized there was someone knocking at my window. I rolled it down, and a cop asked if I was OK. I said sure, and reached for the key. It was already turned, but the car wasn't running.

I got out of the car. I was on the side of the road, maybe a quarter-mile from the parking lot I thought I was in.

As we drove to the police station, the cop said to me, "You know you hit somebody back there." I denied it. I knew I hadn't hit anyone. I wasn't that drunk.

I blew a .284 on the breathalyzer.

Over the next few weeks, I began to recall what happened. I could see someone in the headlight beam. And I could remember staring in the rear-view mirror at a dark shape in the road, pounding on the steering wheel and yelling "Fuck!" over and over until my car slammed into a telephone pole.

I knew the guy I hit. He and I had talked and bought each other drinks for four hours that night. We left the bar together. He said he didn't need a ride home because he lived nearby. He started walking as I went to my car.

They found him right after they found me. He had a concussion, a fractured pelvis and a broken spine. He is a quadriplegic.

I continued to drink. I drank because it helped me forget, and yet drinking made me feel even more guilty.

I still drove drunk. Some mornings I had to look to make sure my car was outside.

I didn't tell my family about the accident for five months. I was afraid to answer the phone. "Fine," I'd say. "No problems," when they did get through to me.

I finally told them a month before I went to court. My lawyer had told me I might have to go to prison.

The night before the trial, I had a few beers.

I was sentenced to two months in the county prison.

When I got out I was determined not to drink. I started watching a lot of TV. I was depressed, and felt sorry for myself. I missed drinking.

I met weekly with a psychologist. He explained that what I felt was grief over the loss of my "best friend" _alcohol.

We talked about the guilt I felt over paralyzing another person, and the latent guilt I felt over dropping out of school.

I told him I couldn't imagine a life without alcohol. He told me that in time I'd find many things to do besides drink. I didn't believe him. He said I should keep seeing him until I didn't have time to anymore.

My lawyer told me the guy I'd hit wanted to see me. I couldn't bring myself to call him. One morning, I opened the paper to a picture of him strapped in his wheelchair. He was speaking at area high schools about drunk driving.

I forced myself to go see him. I had never been more afraid of anyone. I was shaking as I waited in the hospital lobby.

He told me he had been in counseling and wasn't angry anymore. He saw us both as victims of circumstance. He said it was an accident, and that I should forgive myself. He had.

I started doing volunteer work at an adult day-care center. I began taking flying lessons. I started reading books again and keeping a journal. And I enrolled at Temple.

I told my psychologist I just didn't have time for him anymore.

It's been over two years since I had a drink. I can never drink again.

RIDER COLLEGE WOMAN OF THE YEAR AWARD,

December 21, 1989

Ms. Caroline Muka
Student Activities
Student Center

Dear Ms. Muka:

We are pleased to inform you that you have been nominated for the 1989 Rider College Woman of the Year Award.

This will be the fourth annual award presented to honor the one woman member of the staff, faculty, or administration who, through significant college activities and service to the Rider Community, has most effectively created a positive image for women at Rider and thereby contributed to the effort to elevate the status of all women.

The award will be presented on March 14, 1989 at the Women's Studies Colloquium.

The award selection committee requests that you provide information about your activities and achievements related to the award criteria. If you have a current resume, you may wish to attach it. All materials you supple will be confidential.

On the form provided, please provide a statement of how you see yourself as contributing to creating a positive image for women at Rider in an effort to elevate the status of all women. Please do not be modest. Please return this form and related materials to Kathy Holden, Library 231, by January 27, 1989.

Sincerely,
Kathy Holden

Kathy Holden
January 11, 1989
Rider College

Re: Rider College Woman of the Year Award

I have attached the completed forms as requested. Additional information consisting of both On-Campus Activities and also Off-Campus Activities, copies of correspondence from Rider Personnel and newspaper articles pertaining to my activities are included with this application.

Very truly yours,
Carolyn K. Muka

COMMUNIQUE: MUKA NAMED RIDER'S
WOMAN OF THE YEAR 3/13/89

When the Women's Studies Committee presents its Rider College Woman of the Year Award on March 14, they will be honoring more than just one woman.

Carolyn K. Muka, administrative secretary for student services and reservations in the Student Activities Office, and 1989 recipient of the Sadie Ziegler-Bernice Gee Award said, "This award isn't just for me. It's for the union, the clerical level at Rider. It is a boost to all of us. They truly did judge this on who the woman is and not the position or degree she holds."

Carolyn, who has a diploma from Trenton High School, was chosen as "the one woman member of the staff, faculty, or administration who, through significant college activities and service to the Rider community, has most effectively created a positive image for women at Rider and thereby contributed to the effort to elevate the status of all women."

If degree and position weren't the determining factors in Carolyn's selection for the award, it must have been the inner strength that has seen her through numerous personal tragedies.

A YEAR after marrying Leonard L. Muka in November of *1952*, Carolyn gave birth to her first child, a girl, Diana. Three months later, Diana died of Sudden Infant Death Syndrome. Over the next nine years Carolyn had five boys.

In 1979 her eldest son, Stephen, was diagnosed as having Hodgkin's Disease. He underwent numerous operations, chemotherapy and suffered for six years until he died in July of 1985. Six days after the funeral, Carolyn's third son, Michael, was struck by a drunk driver while walking home from work. The accident left Michael a quadriplegic. Sixteen months later, Carolyn's second oldest son, Christopher, was involved in an accident in which a young girl on drugs ran a blinking red light and smashed into the vehicle Christopher was driving, leaving him brain injured. In August of 1987, Carolyn's husband, Leonard, suffered a heart attack and underwent triple bypass surgery.

"For nearly three months after Leonard's surgery, the responsibilities of maintaining my full-time position at Rider, as head of the household, monitoring Leonard's condition at home, monitoring Michael's condition in Philadelphia, as well as caring for Christopher, was totally mine," recalled Carolyn.

CAROLYN attributes much of her ability to come through all this adversity to her mother. "Mom is my role model," said Carolyn of her 77-year-old mother, Marion Callahan. "She helps me keep my head on straight. Mom taught me to always save a piece of yourself. No matter what happens and no matter how much you want to give, you have to keep a piece of yourself for yourself."

Through all of this, Carolyn has maintained a sense of the positive. She beams when she talks about Christopher's progress, her youngest son's, James, flourishing career as a certified public accountant, her second youngest son's, Lawrence, preparations to graduate from Rider, and Michael's ability to make a life for himself.

Last fall, for Rider's Alcohol Awareness Week, Carolyn, Michael and the man who struck Michael, held a program on drinking and driving. It would be easy for Carolyn and Michael to be bitter. Instead, they have taken the man into their hearts and consider him a family friend.

GIVING TO Rider is something Carolyn does regularly. While secretary in the Athletic Department, Carolyn coordinated the Major Gift Fund Drive, leading the department to be the first on campus to achieve 100 percent participation. She is an active member of AFSCME and is currently co-editor of the newspaper and major fund raiser.

Basketball games, both home and away, men's and women's, is where Carolyn can most often be spotted. She was honored by the Lady Broncs in 1983 for her support to the program. That same year the Rider Tang Soo Do Karate Club recognized her for her outstanding support.

In the ten and a half years that Carolyn has been at Rider she has steadily up-graded and improved her secretarial skills. She came to the College in 1978 as a level 2 in the

College Store. In 1981 she became a level 3 in the Athletic Department, and just last June rose to a level 4 in the Student Activities Office. Carolyn admits she came to Rider so her sons could get a college education, but says the friendship and support she has received here mean the most to her.

"I've really been quite a lucky woman to have been here ten years and received this award," said Carolyn. "It's given me such a high."

This is the fourth year the Sadie Ziegler-Bernice Gee Award has been presented. Past recipients are: Eva Krebs, director of judicial and student information systems, 1988; Mary D. Pinney, assistant dean in the School for Continuing Studies, and Dr. Katharine Hoff, professor of English, 1987; and Dr. Virginia Cyrus, director of Women's Studies and associate professor of English, 1986.

The President from Rider College, Frank Elliott, sent me a copy of the "report of the President from 1988-89, 125th Anniversary. With a little stick on a piece of paper he wrote, *Carolyn, check pages 12-13.*

Student personnel and SGA sponsored the most ambitious and successful welcome week program ever. Throughout the year, Family Day's "Mardi Gras," Alcohol Awareness Week's "Drinking and Driving — A Fatal Attraction," and SGS'S "Spirit Semester," Black History Month, and Women's Month all provided quality programs which attracted good attendance and helped increase student esprit. One program during the Alcohol Awareness week was particularly memorable. It involved Carolyn Muka, Administrative Secretary in Student Activities, her son, a quadriplegic who was hit by a drunk driver; and the drunk driver. None of the 300 who attended will ever forget their account of what happened and the impact it has made on their lives, etc. etc.

RIDER COLLEGE – 125th Anniversary

"One of my more memorable and touching experiences at Rider was a program held during Alcohol Awareness Week 1988. Carolyn Muka, her quadriplegic son (a victim of drunk driving) and the drunk driver agreed to tell their story to the Rider College community. How afraid I was that no one would show to hear their powerful message! What a relief and sense of pride I felt to have over 300 people stuff into the Fireside Lounge of the Student Center to hear a very important and painful experience. This was definitely the most satisfying and educational program I have ever coordinated in my professional career."

Cassie Iacovelli,
Director of Student Activities
   Just a few notes: In 1992 the Rider Women of the Year were

Dr. Judith Johnston and Cassie Iacovelli. (Cassie was a former boss of mine at Rider College.)

Rider was good for and good to me. It was Cassie who called Bill Haydasz to tell him that Michael had died on December 5, 1994.

HOUSES

HOMES		YEARS
Leonard's Mother's home, .	Lamberton St., Trenton, NJ	2
Levittown, PA	69 Whitewood Drive	10
Michigan	Utica	1 1/2
Yardley	6 Wilbur Road	17
Ewing/Trenton	Scudders Falls Apartment	4
Hamilton/Trenton	470 Miller Avenue	10
Hamilton/Trenton	Senior Citizen's Apartment	3 1/2
	Long Beach Island	2

TOTAL YEARS 50

Living in Len's Mother's home was very nice for me right off. His sister Mary and his Mother liked me and I liked them. Mary died a few days after Diana was born and then of course Diana died. I always felt that they were in heaven together. After Stephen was born Len and I moved to Levittown, PA where we would not have so many memories.

Levittown was great, with Stephen and his four new brothers, Christopher, Michael, Lawrence and James. (Some how I didn't have any trouble keeping busy.)

When James was just 9 months old, we moved to Michigan where, of course, Leonard had his first heart attack. We had a brand new, big, beautiful home in Utica, Michigan but the heart attack changed everything.

Back east to Yardley, PA right across the bridge from Trenton, NJ. The Yardley home is where we stayed the longest raising our five young sons. (Len went from General Motor's to the bakery in those years.) Boys went to St. Ignatius Grammar School and Bishop Egan High School, and of course, worked in the bakery. We lived right on the corner of Wilbur and Rabb.

Scudders Falls apartments were in Ewing/Trenton, NJ. A lot happened while we lived there. James married Magda, Feather came home to us, Kimberly was born, Stephen died, Michael was hurt, Christopher was hurt.

Things that happened at the 470 Miller Home:

We had to take a wall down between the kitchen and the dinning room to make room for a country kitchen so we could have a nice big table for everyone to eat at and be comfortable.

February 16, 1990 my Mitsubishi was rear ended, my fore-head smacked the steering-wheel even though I had my seat belt on and my black eyes made me look like a raccoon. My poor Mitsubishi with the license plates 'OME OMY' on it looked pretty sad. I still have black floaters in my right eye from that accident and I still have those license plates but now they are on my NEW Buick.

In March of 1993 we had a big snow storm, 10 days later it was Spring. Got some really nice pictures of the house and all the snow and then sunshine.

Mother's Day 1993 Christopher gave me a bird house. It took three men to hang it on the tree in the back yard of 470 Miller. Make that four men, Alexander was in on it also.

Thanksgiving 1993 was the last time Betty came down stairs .

December 15, 1993 Aunt Betty died, December 5, 1994 Michael died, May 1995 my Mother died. Then 1996 was a good year. April 1997 Dick Daly died.

When death is far away we fear him but when he finally comes, he comes as a friend. (I have been with Stephen, Betty, Michael and my Mother the moment they passed, very peacefully and I was one minute away when Dick passed.) I no longer fear death. Frequently I think of death as my friend. In this life, believe me, there are more things to fear worse than death.

At the house on 470 Miller we had a great big kitchen sink. If you wanted a pool at our place, you had to get into the sink. Many a grandchild had a bath in the sink.

In 1994 when I turned 60, my Laura and Magda had my picture taken - one of those where they doll you up, put something fancy on you and take "movie type pictures." I must have liked them because everyone got pictures from me for Christmas that year.

I made the little girls, Darian and Nicholette, beautifully knitted outfits to match (hats, sweaters, leggings and afghans). Darian in white and Nicholette in yellow. I, of course, took pictures of our little girls in their outfits and sent some pictures to the yarn manufacturer. The company was so pleased that they sent me a certificate for free yarn. Later, in a letter from them, they told me to check out their next catalog and sure enough there was a mention of the outfits.

I always took advantage of being as normal as I could. Religion was the best thing I had going for me. I really believed that if God brings you to it he will bring you through it. My only prayer was, "God give me the strength and I will use it." Seems strange, but it was never another prayer. I always left it up to God.

Family, friends, work, sports, etc. I was always busy. That was my answer to almost everything. I was once told by a doctor who did a study on Michael's case, "You must keep a carrot out there in front of Michael so he will want to live." Well guess what? To this day I keep my own carrot out there to keep me through the rough spots, good advice for anyone.

Somewhere around 1995 Leonard and I got this little hot tub for the back deck at 470 Miller Avenue. I can't tell you the times that we had in that tub. Len and I every morning would go out and have our coffee in the warm tub and listen to the radio for the weather and news. What a nice way to start the day. When the grandchildren were over they were always in it. Of course, that meant that they went from the hot tub to the kitchen sink to get rinsed off.

Our back deck was the place to be. Lots of room and a hot tub, (and by the way a red/white strip awning that looked like an ice cream shop, every one of the children wanted to roll the awning in and out but it took a little muscle.) Table and chairs, grill, etc. It was a nice place to have the grandchildren play with things like play dough - easy to cleanup, just get out the hose. Again great pictures, in and out of the hot tub. Darian and Grandmom, Kimberly alone with a hot tub full of bubbles. (Kimberly being the oldest, that was a big privilege to have the hot tub to herself.) One night, when I was baby sitting, I promised Alexander and Nicholette that if they went to bed early, whenever they got up we would go out into the hot tub. Well a promise, is a promise and it was 3 a.m. when they got up, so out we went. We were having such a good time, Alexander started to howl and soon all the dogs in the neighborhood were howling and we had to sneak back into the house. Once when Eliot was just a few months old, and Darian and I wanted to get into the hot tub, I just took Eliot with me and fed him his bottle. (Don't tell Laura but Eliot loved it, and of course he went right from the tub to the sink and got a bath. Great memories.)

When the snow came and the deck out back was piled high with snow, you can be sure that there was a path to the hot tub and the top was all cleaned off. Like I said before, Len and I went in it every morning and the best was when it was cold everywhere else.

I love hats and all through the scrapbooks you will see grandchildren with my hats on. Hats take up a lot of space so I just punch a large nail in my bedroom walls and up goes a hat, just like most people would hang a picture. I know, I know, half of a deck but I LIKE IT.

My favorite pair of eye glasses are my large red- rimmed ones. I think I have a picture of all the grandchildren at one time or another wearing them. I also have all my old records, right down to "Puff the Magic Dragon," when the grandchildren were little it would keep them busy for a little while.

Carolyn Kennedy Muka
470 Miller Avenue
Trenton, NJ 08610
September 8, 1994

Dear President Clinton,

Welcome back from your vacation. Now that you are rested, I need your help. I am a 60 year old woman, a normal married woman with children, grandchildren, etc. I went on a vacation to Nova Scotia, Canada the end of June 1994, ended up in a Canadian Hospital with an asthma attack that would not quit. The tour I was on had to leave me there while they continued on with their trip. I got very good care in that Canadian Hospital, nothing there was pretty or brand new but everything worked. The job was done and they got me back on my feet.

PLEASE, GET OUT YOUR HEAVY GUNS AND GET
THIS HEALTH CARE PACKAGE FOR US PEOPLE.

I have a long list why and I can document each and every thing
I say here. It is a long story but true. My family and many more like
me, as I'm sure you know, need this National Health Care Plan. Being in a Canadian Hospital really brought home to me how it can
and does work.

I have been married for 42 years (11/27/52). My husband is 10
years older and had a triple by-pass in August 1987. For me, it was
a serious back surgery August 1989.

We had six children:

Diana, born 10/3/53 - .died 12/31/53 from SIDS

Stephen, born 10/18/54 - died 7/11/85 from Hodgkin's, he was
a very successful business man in Chicago, went to Deep Springs
College where only the top 1 percent get to go if they are one of
the lucky 30 students. (U.S.Robotics, Chicago Stephen was one of
the founding fathers.)

Christopher, born 12/26/57 - received a bad head injury on
11/26/86 when a drug addict in a stolen car ran a red light and
nearly killed Christopher. Christopher graduated from College with
honors in 1984. Got or will get his FIRST JOB SINCE THE AC-
CIDENT ON OCTOBER 1, 1994...WITH BENEFITS.

Michael, born 8/25/59 - _Walking home was hit by a drunk
driver who left the scene of the accident on 7/22/85. Michael still
lives as a C4 quadriplegic.

Lawrence, born 2/4/61 -_married, 2 daughters, has an inherited
blood problem that was passed on to one of the daughters. Lawrence is a College Grad, works full time.

James, born 12/16/63 - married, 1 son, 1 daughter. James is
College Grad and CPA.

If you look at the dates carefully, you will see that in 16 months
we had three adult sons knocked right out of the ball park. Hodgkin's, Spinal Cord Injury, Head Injury, ALL not their fault. (Six children —2 dead, 2 injured, 2 ok).

We do pretty good, a full and busy life but if the health care and money to pay for health care was not a problem I might even live a little longer myself. One big fear is that my quad will not have proper care if any thing happens to me or his insurance gets used up. This could mean "A ward of the State" as I have been told and will never forget those words.

Remember, I'm just an average mother now 60 years old who 42 years ago married a man 10 years older than herself (Which makes him 71 in October, still working because he and I still need our health insurance).

My only prayer is "God give me the strength and I'll use it." He has and I do. Please stick to your plan and help us people.

Signed
Carolyn Kennedy Muka

THE WHITE HOUSE
WASHINGTON

September 23, 1994

Mrs. Carolyn Kennedy Muka
470 Miller Avenue
Trenton, New Jersey 08610

Dear Carolyn:

Thank you for your thoughful letter. I am deeply touched that you chose to share your personal experience with me.

The hardship and frustration you described illustrate exactly why this nation needs health care reform. At some point during the year 58 million American go without insurance, and each month two million more lose their insurance.

I am committed to achieving health care coverage for all Americans. At the same time, I am working to maintain quality and choice, contain costs, and place a greater emphasis on primary and preventative care. By strengthening what is right in our current system and fixing what is wrong, we can provide the American people with the health security they deserve.

I know that few issues touch the lives and affect the well-being of our citizens more than their health care. As we move forward with Congress on this critical issue, I will keep your experience in mind.

Sincerely,
Bill Clinton

In 1996, while still living at 470 Miller, I was 62. This meant that I could collect Social Security. I took my paperwork to a Buick car dealer and showed him how much I was going to get, told him I didn't want to put anything down, didn't want my payments to go over the amount of this monthly check. (I never had this money before, and before I got used to getting it, I wanted it to go for a NEW car for me.) I ended up with a five-year loan, Buick Century, black cloth top, ruby red bottom, silver luggage carrier on trunk. It took me the five years to pay it off but I never once asked Len for a payment.

Len did not want me to collect my Social Security at 62. He said "Why do you want to do that, you will get all of mine when I die." I felt that I had worked and put that money into Social Security, I had retired, and I wanted the freedom and safety of a NEW car. I am sure that is what Leonard did not want me to have. Remember, I am Irish and it may take me a long time but I will get what I want, even if I was 62 when I finally got THE NEW CAR. Before that, in my life time, Len and the boys bought me a used car once, which they drove into the ground. I have only one memory of ever even driving that car and that was picking up and delivering kids to sports. Then there was the used Mitsubishi that Len bought me that I had only a few months when I was rear-ended and the car was totaled. I must say at this point: Leonard did always pay for the car insurance.

Marlene, Patty and I went to see our brother Jimmy (Martin) in Delaware via the Lewes Ferry in August 1996. I took my brand new car on the ferry and was scared to death that something would happen and it would sink. Of course, it didn't. Jimmy, our sister-in-law Pat, their son Joe, Marlene, Patty and I all went out to lunch that day at Roehova Beach.

MONASTERY OF SAINT CLARE

Thursday, June 20
Dear Carolyn:

Thank you so much for coming to our reunion of May 26, 1996. The news of our happy weekend has traveled far and wide.

The gift you made for the Barber Shop Quartet is beautiful and Buddy was really surprised. I had never told him what it was all this time. He and Al sent me a lovely letter in which you and the gift are mentioned. I will call you and read it to you over the phone.

The Sisters, too, enjoyed it all so much. It was really a fun time shared together. Al sent me the album with the pictures which I think are so good. That day has become a precious memory. Thank you again and again for your presence among us and for all that you contributed. You are a gem.

I talked with Leonard yesterday and he told me you were away. I hope you enjoyed your trip. I hope you will enjoy all your days and years ahead and a long, happy future with your loved ones. You and Leonard and family are remembered in my prayers.

Love,
Sr. Vicky

I had made a blue satin back and stage with 'Three and a half notes' (name of the quartet) in silver glitter. Little blue and white striped bears, singing around a piano. Little white straw hats with red ribbons around the crowns of the hats. All the edges trimmed up with glitter and lace. It was cute and I am sure it ended up in some nursing home or hospital. We did this crazy thing with me unveiling it and then we all sat around and listened to Buddy play a real piano and we all sang. Can you imagine that Buddy and Al came to visit the nuns from Canada and made time for this?

In April 1998, we sold our home at 470 Miller Avenue and put the money on the shore house mortgage. Len and I took an apartment in the Senior Citizen Hamilton Building on the eighth floor. That was great for us because it was no punishment to go to the shore house every weekend (except for the summer when we would rent). This way Len could still keep his State job and keep our health insurance.

Leonard and Uncle Al turned 75 years old in October 1988. Jeff, Marlene, Patty, George, Aunt Pat, Gene, Aunt Helen and I took them out to dinner. Uncle Albert is one day older then Leonard. Let me tell you, that has carried a lot of weight over the years.

I won a District First Award from the New Jersey State Federation of Women's Clubs for a knit adult sweater that I made for myself. It was the first time that I entered anything.

Leonard, Christopher, Lawrence, James and I had to go to Chicago to be deposed in my case against the blood bank that gave Stephen AIDS. Leonard, Christopher and I went to Chicago together and the next day, Lawrence and James went together. On the plane that Leonard, Christopher and I were on, we were delayed for hours. In all, it took us five and a half hours for a two-hour flight. That flight gave me blood clots in my right leg that took the whole summer to clear up. At first, the doctors thought they could do it

131

with meds and at home, after that there was a 10-day stay in Mercer Hospital. Then, the rest of the summer at home with me giving myself an injection of blood thinner - one in the morning and one at night (84 injections in all; I counted them).

NOW, HERE IS SOME REALLY FUN NEWS: LEN, CHRISTOPHER AND I BOUGHT A HOME ON LONG BEACH ISLAND, May 31, 1996. We had to rent it during the season for the next six years, but it was worth it because later we lived in our home on Long Beach Island full time.

Eliot was the first grandchild to ever be in this house. I was baby sitting him while I was looking at it. We have always tried to save some good days for the kids even though we had to rent to keep the house. There were times that Laura, Lawrence, Laura's family, James and Magda even paid rent just so they could use the house during the summer and at that time we really needed the rent. You don't forget things like that. This was our second house and it really stretched us, but OH how happy I am about it.

This is an old, Cape Cod that needed a lot of work. BUT, IT IS THE FOURTH HOUSE FROM THE ATLANTIC OCEAN. We have wonderful neighbors - I like them every one. Of course, everyone is happy when you are down the shore. This little house has two bedrooms downstairs and a dormitory type room for the whole upstairs. The first thing we did was load the upstairs with lots of beds so everyone had a place to sleep.

The second thing was to take the wall down between the kitchen and the living room. Where the wall was we put our dinning room table. We had to put in a new hot water heater, dish washer, washing machine, dryer, outside shower, and a huge beam in the ceiling where we took the wall down to hold the upstairs up. Steps had to be put in the backyard leading up to the deck upstairs.

Now, for about five years we got along with the house like this. Our main address was Trenton and LBI was our second home. Each year we rented the summers and made enough money to pay the mortgage. All the expenses of the house we had to pay but we were glad to do so. I used to have my friends down occasionally on Tuesdays, Wednesdays and Thursdays. This left each weekend for Leonard and Christopher plus, long weekends for family when they got a chance to come down the shore.

A funny story: Leonard was 72 years old when he signed for a 30 year mortgage. James and Magda had wanted to get out of the Town House in Freehold but they didn't think that they wanted to take on a larger mortgage. When James realized that his Father had just signed for a 30-year mortgage, which would make Leonard 102 years old when it was paid off, James and Magda went out and got the home of their dreams.

So now, Laura and Lawrence, Magda and James both have lovely homes with in ground pools in their backyards. The shore is still a drawing card and who wouldn't want to go see Grandmom and Grandpop if you could go out on the beach.

This little house does have a sun-room down stairs and a full bath on both floors. One thing we did do the second year was put in a gas/hot water heating system. That is a blessing because now we have a year-round house.

You name the person and they have been here. I use to do round trips and take the ladies from the senior citizen building to the shore house just to have lunch and get a breath of good sea air. We took drives up and down the island, one day we went to Atlantic City by boat just for fun. I was not always busy with people. I often came down the shore just to be by myself. I would do projects on the house and do a lot of sewing and knitting. I have no problems with my own company. My scrapbooks are full with pictures of good times in this little spot of heaven.

Beautiful Long Beach Island in winter, spring, summer and fall. Even the beach with snow on it and a sled can be a lot of fun.

Every spring we had to get the shore house ready for the renters. Taking out all our personal stuff and making sure every thing was up to snuff. We never had any trouble renting because people loved being so close to the ocean. It was easier on the children and the adults, running off the beach and being so close to the bathroom. Then finally, it would be September again and we would be able to get back into the house and make ourselves at home again.

We have all sorts of pictures with the kids playing, catching sand crabs, digging holes in the sand, painting shells, going crabbing with their parents etc. A lot of good memories. Near LBI is a little sea port in Tuckerton. It is fixed up real nice, and you can take a boat over the bay to the seaport during the season - a nice thing to do for a change, especially when you have company and are looking for something to do.

Remember, we still have our little spring and fall get togethers with all the ladies, the 'Tuesday, Wednesday, Thursday girls' shall survive one way or another.

Most of the time, when I was at the shore alone, I was busy: made corduroy for the boys and velvet for the girls, fur pillows, fur bears, night gowns, pj's, knitted hats, mittens, doll clothes, jackets, afghans, plus all the sewing for the women's club.

Eliot grew to just love Alexander and Alexander just loved Eliot, the oldest grandson and the youngest grandson. Everything Alexander did, Eliot wanted to do. It was nice to see how well they got along when they were together. July 2000 made Eliot the big brother and Nathaniel the little brother in their home. Darian and Nicholette were like twins. When Kimberly was with the gang, she would help keep them out of trouble and that would always make for a nice visit.

We do get snow down the shore and once we got a real dump, so I had to head for Trenton and three days later I came back to the shore and had to leave my car out in the middle of the street because I could not get any closer to the house. It only happened once since we purchased the shore home, most times the snow just gets blown away by all the wind.

The scrapbooks are going a little faster now. The hardest years started in 1978 when Stephen first got sick and I would like to think that they ended in 1994 when Michael died but that isn't so, but close. I don't know if it got easier or if we just handled things better.

Later when we invited our family down for Thanksgiving it

would be from Wednesday night to Sunday afternoon. We finally boiled it down to the weekends (because we could not take our daughters-in-law away from their families all the time). After the holidays we get our whole bunch. It works for us and it works for the in-laws also. Especially at Christmas time, it extends the pleasure of the holidays for us and the children.

There are lots of great pictures of the shore house showing all of the changes plus all of the people who got a chance to spend some time here. I am sorry I never started a 'guest book'. Pictures of sunrises and sunsets. The sun comes up over the ocean and sets down the street over the bay. It doesn't get any better then that. Between the ocean and the bay is only three blocks. It really is an island.

My scrapbooks are filled with lovely letters from our family and friends who have used our shore home. It makes me so happy to be able to share this house with others.

The following is just a sample of the notes we have received:

Hi Carolyn.

Just a note to say "thanks" for a great day I had at your lovely home at the shore. The weather was great, the meal was great, and the people added the final touch. I am glad, that Charlotte and Josephine came along. I know they had a great time as well. I just want you to know, how much I appreciate it, you offering the invitation to join the ladies at your home, and offering me your home for several days is just wonderful. Frank and I are deeply touched, that you have allowed us to enjoy your home as you and your family truly enjoys being there. It is a home, that is filled with so much love and happiness that anyone who walks through that front door feels the joy that is in the house. You are truly a wonderful, caring person, who is so much fun to be around.

Thanks so much.
Love, Carol
From Dot Rettman, Laura's Mom:

AN IRISH BLESSING,

May the road rise up to meet you,

May the wind be always at your back,

May the sun shine warm upon your face,

May the rains fall soft upon your fields,

And until we meet again.

May God hold you in the hollow of his hand.

Len and I moved to the shore home in September 2001 for keeps. For 10 months Len commuted to Trenton each day, all through the winter, leaving in the dark and coming home to LBI in the dark after work, never complaining, because he loves the shore so much. BUT when the nice, beautiful summer days came he could no longer leave the house each morning and retired to enjoy the good life. Len was 80 in October, 2003.

We have our house set up now, that our company can enjoy the up stairs with a sitting/sun room, newly built on the deck upstairs, saving just a bit of outside deck to sit outside. This way, Len and I lived all the time down stairs and got to enjoy everyone, and the company could come and go upstairs by the outside steps and enjoy some privacy. Works for me....

RELATIVES/ FRIENDS

Hamilton Happenings - Mercer Messenger, Thursday, January 28, 1993 had a picture of five Republican Club members, one of them was my brother, Jeff Callahan. The first sentence is: LARGEST REPUBLICAN CLUB - The Hamilton Township recently announced that it is New Jersey's largest Republican Club with over 600 members. (Guess who is the membership chairman? My brother, Jeff.)

My brother Jeff received all sorts of awards for his work in the Republican Club. He is outstanding at getting new members. Never got me though, I am a Democrat through and through. My maiden name is Kennedy. I am Irish, I am Catholic, I am in the working class, so what else would I be but a Democrat?

Marlene (my sister) had a daughter on my birthday February 27 and I had a daughter born on Marlene's birthday on October 3.

During a blizzard, my brother Jeff, who lived only a few doors down the street (470 Miller), made it to our house, FOR A BOTTLE OF WINE. I got a picture of that for sure. Len bought a snow blower after that storm but would you believe it, when the first opportunity came to use it, Len was in Mercer Hospital with another heart attack. We had about four snow storms that year and Len finally got to use the snow blower.

Early August 1989 my brother Martin (Jimmy) and family came to visit. We had dinner at our house. We never get enough time with

137

our brother Martin and family over the years.

Our Mother turned 80 years old in 1991. Mayor Rafferty gave her a chance to sit behind his desk and get her picture taken. He also came to lunch with Mother, Marlene, Patty, Jeffrey and I. It turned out to be very nice and our Mother was proud.

My Uncle Clement and Aunt Mae moved to Sun City in Arizona. At times, Uncle Al and Aunt Helen, plus my Mother would go out to visit. Clem and Mae were happy there except for the hot summers, then they would go on vacation to the mountains of Utah.

My Mother had a Boston Terrier named "Yankee." That dog was really spoiled and my Mother didn't seem to have any trouble with her asthma either.

Martin married a wonderful girl named Patricia Drew. They had four children: Joseph, Carol, Margaret and James. Joe had a dog named "Valentine." Carol married a fellow named Darrel in 1986, with the arrival of Adam Thomas 11/10/89 my brother Martin and Pat became grandparents.

My sister Patty and her husband George Sampson had three children, Albert, Marion and Suzanne. Albert Sampson married Maria Pitale on November 7, 1992. Like her lots and Albert is like another son to me. I went on a cruise with Marion, her daughter Stephanie and her husband Joe, plus Marlene and Patty of course. We went to Bermuda and it was a wonderful experience. Suzanne and her husband Michael have three boys, Christopher, Matthew and Steven.

It is strange how things turn out. My sister Marlene and her husband Arthur Tomczyk (now deceased) had four daughters, Maryanne, Barbara, Nancy and Amy. Maryanne married young and had a nice family. Barbara married Joe Hill and had two sons and a daughter. Up to this date Nancy and Amy are single working gals.

On May 25, 1994 my brother Jeff Callahan graduated from Mercer County Community College. It was great. I took my Mother to graduation and it was a wonderful night for her. She was so proud of Jeffrey. We could not wipe the smiles off our faces.

This was May 1994 my Mother was 83 years old. In May 1995 she died. Jeffrey was around 44 years old. It had been a long, hard struggle for him.

JEFF CALLAHAN
532 Miller Avenue
Hamilton, NJ 08610

Dear "Mother No.2" Carolyn:

Where do I start to say thank you! Every time I enter my apartment I say "thank you Carolyn" for the terrific painting and cleaning job you did for me. As well as when friends stop by, they are absolutely amazed at the wonderful color and how much it appears to be bigger, fresher looking and neater with all things being the same color.

Thank you also for the tiled kitchen, for buying the framed mirrors and thank you Leonard for putting them up.

Thank you also for preparing the appetizer tray when it was Mother's Birthday and supplying of the liquor as well. Your thoughtfulness is appreciated by me more that I can tell you in words.

Thanks for attending my graduation. Without you there I would really have felt bad. When things seemed to go awkward in my life these last few years between my job, the old man who bothered me, pressures of trying to pass my classwork and just keeping my head free of further distress, you were and have always been my "guardian angel." I often really think of how lucky I am to have a sister equally as thoughtful and very much willing to help a brother with yet the same love that a Mother would share with a son.

I know that you do not like to be placed on a pedestal, but in my mind, you sit mighty high! All my friends 'love you.' They are constantly amazed at how well you manipulate all the many responsibilities, liabilities and constant new horizons that you seem to balance daily.

139

I love you and I only wish that I could strike it rich money wise, so that you and your family would not ever have to struggle financially. But until that time arrives, I will try to accommodate you any other way possible. I am very happy to live near you and to be your brother. Thanks for all you and Leonard have done for me.

(signed)
Jeff

On December 16, 1995 my brother Jeffrey had a Holiday Social Dinner at the Old Heidelberg Restaurant, 2430 Hamilton Avenue, Hamilton, NJ . Marlene, Patty and I acted as hostess and it turned out to be a very special evening. Shortly after that, during the night, the whole place burned down to the ground.

In May 1997 our brother Jeff passed and graduated with his license as a mortician. A dream that took him 26 years. CONGRAT-ULATIONS JEFF, and thank you for the beautiful note you sent me. (Carolyn)

Of course that meant another party:
COCKTAIL PARTY FOR JEFF CALLAHAN,
Friday, May 30, 8:30 p.m._
Place: Jerry's, 1701 Hamilton Avenue, Hamilton, NJ.
In recognition of completing the educational requirements for the Funeral Service
Education Program at Mercer County Community College.
RSVP: Carolyn K. Muka.
In October of 1999 my sister Marlene had both of her knees replaced. She did a hell of a job with her recovery because she was going to Europe in six months and she was ready to go when the time came. That 'carrot' out in front again. I really believe in it for everyone.

My sister Patty had a heart valve replacement done at Honnaman Hospital in Philly. It never kept her down. She was off to

Alaska with friend Jo in no time flat after that.

Dr. John Barlow, married to our Aunt Mary Kennedy (Dad's sister) died in 2000. Meant another grave to visit when my sisters and I were at St. Rose of Lima Cemetery. My Mother, my son Stephen, my son Michael, my friend Dick Daly, my Uncle Clement and his wife Mae, my Uncle John Barlow, my Aunt Eleanor, the list goes on and on. The tough part is that I have three sets of old Aunts and Uncles and they are in their 80s now and none of them are in good health. Uncle John Barlow is the first one to pass but in the next few years it is going to be a different story. Even my husband Leonard will be 80. Me, myself and I, of course, have no problems and I am a young 68ish. As of this writing, anyway.

By now my sisters and brother Martin have had grandchildren, all or most of my girl friends are grandparents. What a nice way to slowly slip into middle (old) age. In my scrapbooks I have kept every picture I could get my hands on. Even though there are some that make me sad, there are more that make me happy. (Every two years I bring my scrapbooks up to date). it is a good thing that I have put the names under the pictures, especially when it comes to old neighbors and their children because the old gray matter has a way of letting you down sometimes.

One of my Mother's sayings was, "Remember, wool is warm even when wet."

The following is in honor of Mother because she made beautiful Raggedy Ann dolls. I have one and so do all my brothers and sisters. Now, my daughters-in-law have one of Mother's dolls as a first birthday present when they marry into the Muka family.

RAGGEDY ANN AND ANDY FONDLY REMEMBERED FROM CHILDHOOD

The Times, Sunday, April *15*, 1990 by Linda Rosenkrantz

"CONTEMPORARY COLLECTIBLES"

Ask most people which doll they remember most fondly from their earliest childhood, and chances are that it will be not some fragile blonde beauty with rooted ringlets and icy blue eyes, but one of that cozy, cuddly pair, Raggedy Ann and Andy.

It was ladies first with this duo. Ann was created in *1915,* and cousin Andy followed five years later. They were designed by John (usually referred to as Johnny) B. Gruelle, an Illinois-born cartoonist and illustrator.

According to Susan Ann Garrison, author of the extremely reader-friendly book, "The Raggedy Ann & Andy Family Album," the concept originated when one of Gruelle's children, Marcella, suffering from a serious illness, found an old rag doll in her grandmother's attic. Her father painted a face on it, then named it by combining the titles of two James Whitcomb Riley poems, "The Raggedy Man" and Orphan Annie."

He began to make up stories about the doll to distract the sick child from her misery. When Marcella died in 1916, a year after Gruelle had patented his design, he committed to paper the stories he had been telling her, setting the illustrations in her nursery.

It was the P.F.Volland Co., publishers of his first book, "The Raggedy Ann Stories," who asked Johnny Gruelle if he could make some dolls based on his illustrations to promote the book.

Soon the entire extended Gruelle family: including grandmothers, an aunt and an uncle, were embarked on a cottage industry in an unused Norwalk, Conn., shirt factory, where they made a few dozen dolls based on the old rag doll from the attic.

These early Raggedys, 16 inches long and dressed from the start in cotton pinafores, pantaloons, red-and-white striped leggings and black

Mary Janes, had nondescript brown yarn hair and real candy hearts with the words "I Love You" on them attached to their torsos.

Toward the end of 1918, the Gruelles licensed the Volland Co. to organize a larger scale manufacturing operation. Over time, several different firms were responsible for their manufacture: Mollye's Doll Outfitters produced its version from 1935 to 1938, Georgene Novelties made Raggedys for 25 years, from 1938 to 1962. Other companies making them included Exposition Doll and Toy Co. and American Toy and Novelty Mfg. Co. The Knickerbocker Toy Co. took over in 1962 (changing the hair color from orange to red), continuing until 1983 when the firm was bought by Hasbro, which still produces the dolls today.

Over the years there were many permutations, some more subtle than others. Ann and Andy's eyes have gone from being applied shoe buttons, to painted, to embroidered, to printed. Noses have varied from thin red triangles, sometimes outlined in black, to fat ones. Hair has been brown and red and orange and even blond. Leg stripes have been wide and narrow. And facial expressions have ranged from joy to wonder.

In time, Ann and her nautical cousin were joined by other characters from the books – there have been several dolls of Beloved Belindy and the Camel with the Wrinkled Knees as well.

The story of these American icons is presented in full in Susan Ann Garrison's colorful "The Raggedy Ann & Andy Family Album" 144 pages, with hundreds of color photos to document the changes and variations in the dolls, as well as other Raggedy Ann and Andy products, including story books, dishes and toys.

Linda Rosenkrantz edited Auction magazine and authored five books, Copley News Service, San Diego, CA.

The Archdiocese of Detroit, Parochial Schools, Award of Honor, presented to Stephen Muka for High Scholarship in Grade six for the marking period ending January 28, 1966. Mrs. Cutway, Teacher...(Stephen gave this award to Aunt Betty and Grandmom Muka).

CAROLYN means "Song of Joy" The Lord is my rock,
my fortress, and my deliverer; my God is my rock,
in whom I take refuge. (from Margie Kratzer '93).

Uncle John Muka (Leonard's brother) died on Diane Muka's birthday 10/3 and Diane (Leonard's daughter) died on Uncle John's birthday 12/31.

We had a 70th birthday party for Aunt Betty in 1991. In her younger years she was called Rich Aunt Betty, then Aunt Betty then. Old Aunt Betty. Talk about smiles. She had a great one. I loved her, the whole family loved her. She got to see Alexander, Darian, (Laura and Lawrence's first child) and Nicholette, James and Magda's little girl baby. Days before Betty died she was still smiling. Finally, when she could not talk, nor could she smile, she would just wink.(In the scrapbooks you will find pictures of Betty taking her radiation treatments, needles, etc. She was swell. She would let me do anything to her, just go along with it. We made as much fun doing what had to be done as we could).

Cousin Margie Kratzer was a big help to me with taking care of Aunt Betty. Margie, GOD BLESS HER, when things got real bad, would show up each night, just about the time Leonard would be getting home from work and I would have dinner ready, BUT Margie would not come to eat with us. She would go straight up to Betty. Margie would get Betty ready for the night, keep her company, say the rosary with her, etc. (Thanks Margie, I could never forget what you did for Betty and me.)

December 1991

Dear Leonard AND Carolyn,

This card does really express how I feel. But I still want to say in my words how much I appreciate all that you are doing for me. The good company, meals and time spent going with me to the hospital. It just makes me feel like the most Blessed women in the world! God is really good to me for having you as my family

It has made me very happy and easy also to accept this illness. Thank you so very much and May God Bless You Always. You and the whole family are always in my prayers.

I Love You All!!!

Merry Christmas and a Happy Healthy New Year!

(signed)
Betty

Aunt Betty was 72 when she passed. She had a little canker sore on her tongue. Asked several doctors about it but no one thought it was anything. It took three years, two operations, radiations, lost of taste and smell to kill her. But in the end it did kill her, the BIG C.

Cousin Pete Kratzer, with the help of his wife Margie played Santa in 1990 at a Christmas party Aunt Betty, Leonard and I pulled off, again with the help of everyone. This party brought together, all the families, it was very, very special.

Our list of people who have passed still grows. Our Santa "Peter Kratzer" died in December 1991 never made it to the next Christmas after our family party in 1990.

Mary, Betty, John, and Stephen, Leonard's sisters and brothers are gone. Father Bakaisa, a priest friend of the Muka family has passed also.

WHAT CANCER CANNOT DO
CANCER IS SO LIMITED

IT CANNOT CRIPPLE LOVE,

IT CANNOT SHATTER HOPE,

IT CANNOT CORRODE FAITH,

IT CANNOT DESTROY PEACE,

IT CANNOT KILL FRIENDSHIP,

IT CANNOT SUPPRESS MEMORIES,

IT CANNOT SILENCE COURAGE,

IT CANNOT INVADE THE SOUL,

IT CANNOT STEAL ETERNAL LIFE,

IT CANNOT CONQUER THE SPIRIT.

Author unknown

Len has had two sisters and two brothers die of cancer: Mary, Betty, Stephen and John.

In the spring of 1994, after Betty Muka's death, I took all of her important papers, pictures, etc. and put her whole life into five scrapbooks. After that, the scrapbooks went the rounds of all her friends and *family* to go through. Some wrote little comments, under the pictures. (I always enclosed a pen so they would feel free to write). Next is a note from Sister Vicky from the "Poor Clares" in Bordentown, NJ. It was her nephew that we (Betty, Mary Stercula, Alma DelFavero and I went to see in Toronto).

146

MONASTERY OF SAINT CLARE
201 CROSSWICKS STREET
BORDENTOWN, NJ 08505

Tuesday, May 10
Dear Carolyn:

The albums you put together of Betty's life are a treasure. They brought back so many precious memories. I was deeply moved. Mary Stercula brought them over and I put them on display for all the sisters to see. They truly enjoyed them.

Our Monday Night prayer group was here last night and they looked through the albums with great interest. We saw the pictures of your Toronto trip and all the signatures, etc. What a great piece of work you did. We commend you highly for such love and devotion. Everyone thinks so highly of you for your beautiful relationship and caring for Betty. I know she is interceding for you and your loved ones. Be assured that you, Leonard and your family are always in our prayers.

Love and Prayers,
Sr. Vicky
(I was so moved by all you had of ME in the albums).

Aunt Betty left two wing-back chairs. I got a new couch and bought more material to match the couch.

Our Father John R. Muka (Leonard's cousin) celebrated his 60th anniversary in the priesthood of the Catholic Church on June 20, 1999. Len and I (along with Margie Kratzer) got to go and be with him and all his family and friends.

The last of the Opsuth orphans passed away in June of 1999. Evelyn Muka's (Len's sister-in-law,) daughter Elaine M. Welsh passed on October 15, 1998. Evelyn's two sons are doing nicely:

Ricky with wife Patty have two sons and one daughter; Ronald is still single.

SS.Peter & Paul Parish in Trenton, NJ celebrated its 100 anniversary in 2000. This is the parish that Leonard was born into. Leonard's Mom and Dad did a lot to get this Slavic parish going. It used to have a school but that has been closed and taken away but the old stone/brick church is still there up and running. Our Stephen was baptized there and he was also buried there.

I have many dear friends from Rider College. My friend Micky had a place down Long Beach Island. She, especially during the bad times, would have me down with other Rider ladies and they helped me a lot with their support. Later in years, my Mother and I would rent a week in the spring and a week in the fall (cheaper then during the season). We would always rent the same place right on the beach, 5101 Ocean Blvd. There would be a few quiet days for just Mother and me, then it would end up open house. By then my Mother would make me take her home. Mother could never understand me, how I liked people. She was a very private person and I think there were times she didn't even want more than one of us, her own children around. It got so that I would not let Mother chip in on the rent, but I would still do it, this way we would have our quiet days and I could still have my family and friends without feeling bad for Mother.

(We never called our Mother, Mom). My Mother once said to me, "I can't stand it, you are just like the Kennedys, you like children." Man, it took me awhile to figure that one out, but I finally did and I didn't like the answer.

I must say though, Mother would always welcome Michael and Christopher. It is a shame that you had to be disabled for her to show any affection. This brings to mind that one day when I was taking my Mother out after Michael's death, I was talking to her about Michael while I was driving and she said, "Get off that Carolyn, for crying out loud. Michael's been dead six months now." IT HAD BEEN SIX WEEKS AND I WAS SUPPOSED TO BE OVER IT ALREADY. You see, it was taking attention away from her, attention she felt that she well deserved. The same with company, you just couldn't have company and my Mother, too.

Trouble is, I am 90 percent like my Mother so I have to watch it and work doubly hard at some of her mistakes so I don't make the same ones. I'm sure I am just making other ones. Oh well, that's life. Please forgive me kids, but remember the word "unyielding?" That is my middle name.

I have lots of pictures from those times in that rented house, good times. Pictures of Mother, my brother Jeff flying a kite on the beach, Aunt Betty, Mike Austin, Michael, Christopher, Leonard, Dick Daly, (Len and Dick took the door off on the rented place so Michael could get through it in his wheel chair. This was after the neighbors had helped us get Michael up the four stairs and onto the deck), Aunt Marlene, Aunt Patty, Pat Johnson, Jo Comber, Agnus, Barbara, Ruth, Mary Lou, Elly, Laura, Lawrence, Darian, Magda, James, Alexander, Nicholette, etc. NOT ALL AT ONCE, OF COURSE, but they were good days.

There were times that Michael and Mike would come down to fish at the Barnigat Light area and they would stop by and I would have their lunches all packed and off they would go.

On Friday, July 27, 1984, some friends and I had a "doggie shower" for our friend Eleanor Curcio of Lawrenceville, NJ. An article and picture appeared in the Times:

ELEANOR CURCIO was a little overwhelmed by the gifts she received at a "Puppy Shower" staged by her friends, Julia Snyder, Bertha Ropeik, Mima Kushner and Carolyn Muka, at the Trenton Country Club. Ms. Curcio had a lifelong fear of animals, but her friends persuaded her to get a dog – she got a Llhasa Apso. "Confucius" is his name. Some of the gifts were, puppy piddle pads, pooper scooper, bumper sticker, doggy goodies to eat etc. Fun was had by all.

We have many nice friends from Rider College. One of our dear friends is Agnus McGlade Berenato, Women's Head Coach for Rider and now Women's Head Coach for the Georgia Tech Basketball Team. Somehow, she had four beautiful children while holding down her job at Georgia Tech. Her husband is really a hell of a guy. Ruth Purcelli and I have a dear friend in common and her name is Norma, but that is another book to be written.

I still have a note from my friend Barbara Cole. One night, right after Michael's stroke, Len and I were coming home late and tired. Low and behold we opened the fridge and there was all sorts of good food already prepared with a note from Barbara.

"Had you on my mind. Hope everything will be OK _ How about pasta and salad for dinner?

Love, Barb.

At this point I would love to mention all our friends but will not, in the event I miss someone. (Besides the list is quite long.) Over the years some of my sisters' friends are now my friends and now they have Rider friends. It's a wonderful circle.

Dot, Laura's Mom left a note at the shore house for me:

"ABOUT THE IRISH"

What shall I say about the Irish -
The utterly impractical, never predictable Irish.
Strange blend of shyness, pride and conceit,
And stubborn refusal to bow to defeat -
He's spoiling and ready to argue and fight.
Yet the smile of a child fills his soul with delight.
His eyes are the quickest to well up in tears,
Yet his strength is the strongest to banish your fears.
And there's no middle ground on which he will stand.
He's wild and he's gentle, he's good and he's bad.
He's proud and he's humble, he's happy and sad.
He's in love with the ocean, the earth and the skies.
He enamored with beauty wherever it lies.
He's victor and victim, a star and a clod -
But mostly he's Irish - in love with his God.

The Mother of a good friend of ours, Gordon Graves, died. He had spent a lot of time with her during her illness in Florida. When the time came and Gordon's Mom died, Gordon had just gotten back home from Florida, so his father, sister and brother took care of everything and Gordon chose not to go back. Everyone was fine with this arrangement. BUT somehow it just didn't set well with Gordon himself, being an odd sort of fellow. (Len and I had met Gordon's Mom on several occasions and liked her very much). Well, Len, a friend Richard F. Daly, and I decided to have a wake for Gordon's Mom and bring everything out in the open and finally help Gordon get over his bad feelings. Now, you must remember that Gordon really is a strange fellow and we knew he would appreciate this:

LIVE FROM BEAUTIFUL HAMILTON TOWNSHIP,
IT'S FRIDAY NIGHT LIVE
Featuring: "GORDO THE MAGNIFICENT" and
THE NEVER READY FOR PRIME TIME
BOARD MEMBERS. The Old Guard From Silver City -
also - A MEMORIAL SERVICE
FOR:MARY MARGARET GRAVES
And now heeeeeeeeeeeeeeeeeeeeeeeeeere's G 0 R D 0!

A Memorial service for the late Mrs. Mary Margaret
Graves will be held on Friday afternoon, April 20, 1990
at the residence of Carolyn and Leonard Muka, 470
Miller Avenue, Hamilton Township, New Jersey com-
mencing at 5 p.m.

Mr. Graves is survived by two sons and one daughter in-
cluding "Gordo the Magnificent" of Lawrenceville, New
Jersey. Gordo is a member of the "Old Guard" of Rider
College.

In lieu of religious services, the Old Guard will hold
a big blast under the direction of Richard F. 'Dickie'
Daly, known as 'God' by his cronies. Friends may call
between 5 and 9 at the Muka residence. The weekly
meeting of the 'board' will be held during this time.
Arrangements are under the direction of Jeff 'Digger
0 Dell' Callahan.

A good time was had by all including Gordon, his friends
around him was all he really needed. Somewhere along the way,
Gordon Graves turned 50. Once again he was at the mercy of his
friends. A party at Rider College was very nice, BUT when he woke
up the day of:

A large sign on his front lawn

'OVER THE HILL'
WITH THE COMPLIMENTS OF LEONARD

for all to see. And Gordon lived on a very busy highway.

Dear Carolyn:

Here it is the start of a new decade and I'm only four months late with this "thank you note". You probably have forgotten what its for. Well I haven't. I want to thank you from the bottom of my heart for helping me celebrate my 50th birthday, with a surprise party.

You can have no idea how touched I was by the number and quality of the people present. In working at a place as long as I have, there is a tendency to get lost in your life and not understand how people care about you. To see the cross-section of the College represented at my party was truly moving. To have the good friends and acquaintances that I have makes me a very rich man indeed.

I face 50 and beyond with both fear and anticipation. The fear is that life passes too quickly, and yet I anticipate what lies ahead. Thank you once again for the gift of your presence and respect. I remain both humbled and honored. I shall cherish the memory for many years.

(Then Gordon wrote by hand)

I knew if I waited long enough, I could kill two birds with one stone. This is a combination thank you for my 50th surprise party, and in recognition of Rider Woman of the Year, my present to you.

Words do not adequately express my feeling for your efforts regarding the party. Just know I was touched deeply by the sentiment and number of people who showed up. Somewhere along the line I must have done something right.

Finding a suitable present, for your honor, was difficult, but the Eagle Proof Coin seemed appropriate. The woman on the coin with outstretched hand seems in keeping with your spirit of helping others. Thank you again for being such a good friend.

Love,
Gordon

Gordon Graves finally retired in 1992. He is with his friend Phillys and they live in Maryland. Of course, another big party only this one Rider put on for Gordon.

There were happy times and there was very sad times. Dick Daly had come to live with Len and I, in that by now famous apartment upstairs. April 30, 1997 he moved his car from our drive way out back, to the front of the house and never made it. A massive heart attack and he was gone. His car drove right up on a neighbor's lawn and stopped when it hit their house. Death was that quick. We lost a dear friend, whose place in our lives will never be filled again.

TRIPS, TRIPS AND MORE TRIPS

TRIPS: New Jersey, Pennsylvania, Michigan, Illinois, Arkansas, Tennessee, Massachusetts, Vermont, New York, New Mexico, Arizona, Nevada, Missouri, Indiana, Ohio, Nova Scotia, England, Bermuda, Canada. There may be more, but not less.

The end of July 1991 Leonard's sister Betty, two friends and I drove to Toronto all by ourselves. We each took turns, two hours at the wheel. Great fun. Betty, Mary, Alma and I got to see Niagara Falls. Friends Buddy and Al just took us under their wings and we really saw a great many things. We still talk about it. (Betty passed away in 1993 and I don't get to see Mary much anymore, but Alma and I see the most of each other.) We even got our picture taken with the Toronto Blue Jays while we were there. We stood on home plate. We learned to take the subway and even the trolley. The only thing on the whole trip that we had a problem with was none of us had ever pumped our own gas for the car, every time it was done it was a real event. We went 1,370 miles. We were so pleased with ourselves that we were not fit to live with for awhile. Just ask, we will be glad to tell you about it.

Patty, Marlene, Jo Comber and I took a day trip to Lancaster County, Hershey, Bethlehem, PA, and we got to see the "CHARLES DICKENS VICTORIAN CHRISTMAS" and heard THE SPOKEN WRITINGS OF EDGAR POE. What a day!

We also have gone on some nice trips. We went to Salem, Mass.

and the Pine Grove Dude Ranch a couple of times. Can you picture 60+ women on horses? It was fun.

Just ran across pictures of our rental at Long Beach Island from September 1994. One with Aunt Patty and Michael out on the deck with the ocean in the background. We had a lot of hard times but we sure did pack in a lot of good times.

Now, I am beginning to think that it was the people around me who kept coming up with ways to make life enjoyable. All I know is that I am not a martyr, never was and never will be. Just remember that carrot you hang out in front to keep you going.

You have to throw in that Pinegrove Dude Ranch every once in awhile. Man I loved that place. (Pat J., Agnus, Mary Lou, Jo, Barbara, Patty, Marlene, Ruth, Elly, etc and me..).

I never tried to escape, truly I carry everything with me. And the longer you carry it the easier it gets. I never tried to run away from any problems. If people could just learn to live with their problems, try to do their best to improve them but keep them with you. That's what makes you whole. Some people feel they want to forget, you can't really forget so don't even try. Remember everything, embrace it, love it, live with it and guess what? You'll come out on top, I promise.

All during those Rider years, when we could, Len and I would follow the basketball of Rider College, both men and women. We would go on some of their away games also. Our family came first but our social life had a lot to do with Rider Sports. Also it helped us be as normal as possible through some tough times. Rider College was very supportive of our family.

In July of 1994 I went to Nova Scotia with my sisters Marlene and Patty, also our dear friend Jo Comber (by now Jo is just one of the sisters). A few days into our 10-day trip I came down with a bad asthma attack and the bus trip had to continue on with out me. Leonard came all the way to Nova Scotia to bring me home after I got out of the hospital. (I have had a hard time getting out of the house since. Len makes me get my doctor's permission each time I decided I HAVE to go somewhere.) Len did have to pay for his own airfare and that was never going to happen again.

Cape May 1995, Laura and Lawrence, James and Magda took places for the same week, for a vacation. Laura invited her parents and Magda invited Leonard, Christopher and me to spend the week with them. It turned out to be very nice. First thing Len did was get lost finding a parking place. He dropped us off at the right place and then Len was off and running. My favorite pictures of Nicholette are from that condo in Cape May. One wall was all mirrors and that is where I got three good pictures of Nicholette and her twin, in Grandmom's cowboy hat. Christopher, Leonard and I went on one of those Whale Watching trips. We actually saw some to my surprise.

Shortly after the death of my Mother, my friend Ruth Purcelli and I went on a trip to Colonial Williamsburg and to Busch Gardens. We had a very nice time and Ruth was a dear, she let me talk the whole time about my Mother. I had the tickets for Mother and me but when Mother passed, Ruth came with me. Like I said, Ruth is a DEAR.

In January 1996 the Trenton area had a blizzard, one for the record books. After the snow was under control, in February our whole family went to the mountains for a skiing trip. Eliot was just a little baby. Almost every time you looked out the windows you could see deer. We kept the fireplace going the whole time we were there - it was one of those big, old, stone fireplaces. Got a lot of pictures on that trip, but I like the ones of Lawrence and James always bringing in the wood.

March 1996 brought me to London with Marlene, Patty and Jo. We did so many things there, but when you look at the pictures I took in every one of them we had our winter coats on. So no matter what clothes we brought with us it still was the same old winter coats in all of the pictures. We went to: Madam Tussaud's wax figures, Buckingham Palace, Canterbury, White Cliffs of Dover, Tower of London, York, Cambridge, Edinburgh, Harrod's department store, Old Roman Fortress, Bath, Big Ben, Thames River, etc. We did three night walks: Ghost, Pub and Jack the Ripper, I really liked that stuff. We stayed at the: Regents Park Marriott. On our tours we ended up using unisex toilets (this I had never seen before), also we had gotten our train passes in the US so off we went on the BritRail and we saw a lot, that plus the Underground, plus the buses, our feet, etc. We really got around. Every place had a gift shop and we did not miss many of them.

It was a shock when after checking into the Marriott and getting a quick lunch that first day, of a hamburger and fries, we came out into the lobby again and saw the headlines of the local news paper: "Mad Cow Scare." Oh well, what is done is already done but we did not eat beef the rest of our time in Britain.

Easter of 1996 at our home on Miller Avenue everyone got their little gifts from London.

There was a Disney trip to Florida taken by: Ted and Dot, Lawrence and Laura, James and Magda and Kimberly, Alexander, Darian, Nicholette, and little Eliot. It was Disney's 25th anniversary and a they had a good time. They took lots of pictures for me. I was supposed to go on this trip but did not feel well, so Dot and Ted went to help with the children. In the end, Dot and Ted were sick part of the trip with the same thing I had.

Long Beach Island rental again, if only Patty would stop feeding those sea gulls. We all got to enjoy Long Beach Island so much that there were times in the winter we would just go for a ride and visit the Atlantic Ocean.

After buying the shore house I thought I would not be taking any more trips, well that didn't last very long: Trip to Branson, saw Mel Tillis, Lawrence Welk's Family show, Yakov Smirnoff, Wayne Newton, Imax Theater, Tony Orlando and Bobby Vinton. It was early November and these were mostly their Christmas shows. Early December these artists take their shows to Las Vegas, so it was very good entertainment. Got to go up into the Gateway Arch in St. Louis - unforgettable.

Patty and Jo took a trip to Alaska the Summer of 1997, so in stead of Marlene and I staying home and feeling sorry for ourselves we took a two-day trip to Gettysburg, PA. A lot of history there and it was the first time for the both of us to see everything. Marlene and I of course, sent cards to Patty and Jo's homes saying, "Wish you were here."

Talk about the carrot - in the last of April and early May 1998, Marlene, Patty, Jo and I went to Las Vegas. Jo had gotten a time-share place from where she worked and we did not have to pay for it. We did them a favor by not letting it go to waste. So we had a week in this really great house, pool, hot tub, etc. We rented a car and went to: St. Joseph, Husband of Mary Roman Catholic Church, Buon Appetito Spaghetteria, Hoover Dam, Lake Mead Cruise, the Red Mountains, the Excalibur, Rio Casino Resort, Mirage, Imperial Palace, Treasure Island, Harrah's, New York, New York Riviera, LaCage, Flamingo Hilton, Luxor, Monte Carlo, Golden Nugget, Stratosphere, Caesars Place, Imperial Palace. (Ask me any questions.) We got to see some shows, too.

In the fall of 1998 it was the Pine Grove Dude Ranch again. 'HOW DEEEEEEEEEEE.'

In July 1999 I brought my friends Ruth and Norma to upper New York State to visit Norm's sister-in-law Dot. We had such a good time. Dot invited us back, and of course, we did go back the following year. Never invite me unless you mean it because I will come. Their family's name is Van De Carr, well known from whence they come. We saw: the St. Charles Hotel in Hudson, NY, Michaels, Tanglewood, Country Curtains and the Red Lion Inn in Stockbridge, Massachusetts, The Norman Rockwell Museum, etc. The second time Ruth, Norma and I got to Dot's we visited a lot of their relatives. Also, we went to see Hyde Park where the Roosevelts lived.

In October 2000 Marlene, Patty, Jo and I went to Oakridge, Tennessee to visit Patty's sister-in-law, Patricia, (George's sister). Man, did we have a good time. We were there a total of 10 days, but a few days we went traveling around and saw: St. Mary's Catholic Church, Oak Ridge, AMSE in Oak Ridge, a dam near by, Grand Resort Hotel & Convention Center, Biltmore Estate, Great Smoky Mountains train ride, Old Harmony Graveyard, DOLLY WOOD,

Dixie Stampede, the Kingdom Heirs, Blont Mansion, Knoxville, the Soup Kitchen, Museum of Appalachia, Tennessee Fall

Homecoming, Rock City, Ruby Falls, Incline Railway, Chattanooga Choo choo, and WAL MART a dozen times. (private joke).

In 2000 at Christmas time, Pat Johnson, Marlene, Patty and I went to NY to see the Rockettes, and then to "Broadway Joe's Steakhouse" for dinner. It was a senior citizen trip and turned out to be a great day.

In the Spring of 2001 Laura had a business trip in Florida and of course, her husband and children just had to join her there to keep her company. Man, Nathaniel was not even a year yet and he had already been to Disney.

Just for the record, there were other good times. These trips just come to mind because I have pictures in the scrapbooks to remind me, (Leonard never paid for any of my trips, nor did he ever want to come with me. It worked for me.)

Carolyn at 60

LAST PAGE

COUNTING COUP

To know that I have honored my words with my deeds,

Sweet Victory is shared by all,

In filling other's needs.

Humankind rejoices! The prize of Counting Coup,

Harmony and balance, A peaceful world anew.

VICTORY

(Leonard L. Muka passed March 19, 2008)

Printed in the United States
208247BV00001B/55-156/P